A CHECKLIST OF
ONTARIO
FRESHWATER FISHES

NICHOLAS E. MANDRAK
AND
E. J. CROSSMAN

A CHECKLIST OF ONTARIO FRESHWATER FISHES

ANNOTATED WITH DISTRIBUTION MAPS

RŌM
Royal Ontario Museum

First published in 1992 by
Royal Ontario Museum
100 Queen's Park
Toronto, Ontario
M5S 2C6

Canadian Cataloguing in Publication Data

Mandrak, Nicholas Edward, 1963-
  A checklist of Ontario freshwater fishes

Includes bibliographical references and index.
ISBN 0-88854-402-2

1. Freshwater fishes - Ontario - Identification.
2. Freshwater fishes - Identification.
I. Crossman, E. J., 1929-   . II. Royal Ontario
Museum.   III. Title.

QL626.5.05M36 1992   597.092′9713   C92-094512-0

ROYAL ONTARIO MUSEUM PUBLICATIONS IN LIFE SCIENCES

The Royal Ontario Museum publishes books on a variety of topics in the life sciences, including Life Sciences Contributions, a numbered series of original scientific publications. All manuscripts considered for publication are subject to the scrutiny and editorial policies of the Life Sciences Editorial Board, and to independent refereeing by two or more persons, other than museum staff, who are authorities in the particular field involved.

Nicholas Mandrak is a Ph.D. candidate in the Department of Zoology, University of Toronto, and the Department of Ichthyology and Herpetology, Royal Ontario Museum.

E. J. Crossman is curator in the Department of Ichthyology and Herpetology, Royal Ontario Museum, and Professor of Zoology in the Department of Zoology, University of Toronto.

The Royal Ontario Museum is an agency of the Ontario Ministry of Culture and Communications.

Cover: *Lepomis gibbosus*, pumpkinseed, from Scott and Crossman, *Freshwater Fishes of Canada*, by permission of the authors.

TABLE OF CONTENTS

Introduction   1
  History of the Knowledge of Composition and Distribution of the
  Fish Fauna   1
Materials and Methods   6
  Distribution Database   6
  Distribution Maps   6
Results and Discussion   8
  Fish Fauna   8
  Distribution of Sampling Sites, 1900–1986   9
  Species Distribution Maps   12
Checklist of Ontario Freshwater Fishes   13
Distribution Maps of Ontario Freshwater Fishes   21
Acknowledgements   162
Appendix 1   Changes in the Scientific Names of Ontario Freshwater Fishes
              since 1980   163
Appendix 2   Instructions on Preparing and Forwarding Information on the
              Ontario Fish Fauna   163
Literature Cited   165
Index to Scientific and Common Names   170

INTRODUCTION

One of the most fundamental and important features of a biological population is its distribution in space. A true awareness of the extent and pattern of distribution of a species is critical to an understanding of its evolutionary history. For freshwater fishes in northern North America, present-day patterns of distribution are the result of processes active following the Wisconsinan glacial period, from 100,000 to 14,000 years ago. During the maximum extent of the Wisconsinan ice sheet, there were no known freshwater habitats in what is now Ontario. The fishes that occurred in Ontario prior to the Wisconsinan glacial period either perished or moved into refuges south and east of the ice sheet. The fishes that occur naturally in Ontario today populated, or repopulated, the existing waters created by the meltwaters of the receding glacial ice. The present-day distributional patterns of fishes can be used to interpret the location of the Wisconsinan refuges and the aquatic pathways available for the postglacial colonization of the newly-formed waterbodies (see Mandrak, 1990). On a practical basis, knowledge of the composition and distribution of fishes is required by those responsible for the protection and management of our aquatic ecosystems. This baseline information is necessary to monitor and assess the human impact on aquatic environments. Anglers using these resources for recreation must be able to determine the location of targeted species.

History of the Knowledge of Composition and Distribution of the Fish Fauna

An account of freshwater fishes of Canada published by Richardson in 1836 was likely the beginning of a recorded inventory of Ontario fishes that continues to this day. After the pioneering work of Richardson, the knowledge of the number of fish species occurring in Ontario gradually developed as a result of the publication of various ichthyofaunal lists for North America, Canada, and Ontario (Table 1), as well as lists documenting regional and local ichthyofaunas within Ontario (Table 2). Selected regional and local works are included for readers interested in published lists for specific areas and in the historical development of this knowledge for certain areas. Hubbs and Brown (1929) recognized both the utility of faunal inventories in attempting to explain the nature of species distributions, and the difficulty of compiling such inventories for Ontario because of its vast area.

The number of species and the number of species records used to map the distributions of Ontario fishes in a variety of publications has increased over the years at a variable rate. A simple numerical expression of the number of records is a mean value derived by dividing the number of species records available (at the time of publication of maps) by the number of species involved.

1

TABLE 1. Number of species recorded for Ontario in publications from 1836 to 1991. Note that number of species is based on species considered valid at the date of publication. Some of these publications include species no longer considered valid.

Reference	No. of Species
Richardson, 1836*	32
Wright, 1892	62
Evermann and Goldsborough, 1907*	52
Nash, 1908	112
Halkett, 1913*	104
Hubbs and Brown, 1929	96
Radforth, 1944	122
Dymond, 1947	117
Scott, 1954	135
Scott, 1958	131
Slastenenko, 1958*	117
Scott and Crossman, 1962	133
Scott, 1963	135
Scott and Crossman, 1969*	135
Scott and Crossman, 1973a*	132
Scott and Crossman, 1973b*	139
Crossman and Holm, 1978	143
Lee et al., 1980**	140
Dodge et al., 1984	152[+]
This study	165[++]

    *   number of species recorded in Ontario as part of a list of freshwater fishes in Canada

  **   number of species recorded in Ontario as part of a list of freshwater fishes in North America

   +   includes four subspecies and one selected hybrid

 ++   includes five subspecies and two selected hybrids

TABLE 2. Selected publications containing lists of freshwater fishes for specific localities within Ontario.

Reference	Locality
Agassiz, 1850	Lake Superior
Ure, 1858	Toronto
Small, 1883	Ottawa
Meek and Elliott, 1899	Muskoka
Meek and Clark, 1902	Lake Simcoe to Lake Superior
Evermann and Latimer, 1910	Lake of the Woods
Nash, 1913	Toronto
Bensley, 1915	Georgian Bay
Dymond, 1922	Lake Erie
Dymond, 1926	Lake Nipigon
Dymond and Hart, 1927	Lake Abitibi
Dymond et al., 1929	Lake Ontario
Toner, 1933	Georgian Bay
Toner, 1937	Eastern Ontario
Dymond, 1939	Ottawa Region
Dymond and Scott, 1941	Northern Ontario
Lindeborg, 1941	Quetico Provincial Park
Curran et al., 1947	Lake Opinicon
Hubbs and Lagler, 1964	Great Lakes
Ryder et al., 1964	Northern Ontario
MacCrimmon and Skobe, 1970	Lake Simcoe
Macins, 1972	Lake of the Woods
Berst and Spangler, 1973	Lake Huron
Christie, 1973	Lake Ontario
Hartman, 1973	Lake Erie
Lawrie and Rahrer, 1973	Lake Superior
Martin and Fry, 1973	Lake Opeongo
McAllister and Coad, 1974	Capital Region
Crossman, 1976	Quetico Provincial Park
Crosman and Van Meter, 1979	Lake Ontario
Coad, 1987	Ottawa District
Strickland, 1988	Algonquin Provincial Park
Hartviksen and Momot, 1989	Thunder Bay

Radforth (1944) was the first to map the distribution of Ontario fishes. The mean number of records per species for these maps is 20. The records of the Royal Ontario Museum (ROM) were plotted manually on a base map of Ontario. Radforth provided maps depicting the distribution of 117 species, and one group of whitefishes represented as *Leucichthys* spp. Since Radforth's publication, the knowledge of the composition and distribution of the Ontario fish fauna has vastly increased through the continued work of the ROM and the National Museum of Canada (NMC) (now called the Canadian Museum of Nature), and through an enormous increase in sampling effort resulting from the advent of the Ontario Ministry of Natural Resources (OMNR) Lake Inventory in 1968 and Stream Inventory in 1971 (Fig. 1). The decline in number of records after 1973 resulted from a steady reduction in activity associated with the OMNR Inventory programs. The number of species records for the last point at which complete data were available (1985) was 1208.

Scott and Crossman (1973a) mapped the distributions of 131 Ontario species and 1 subspecies on a base map of Canada. The known ranges of the

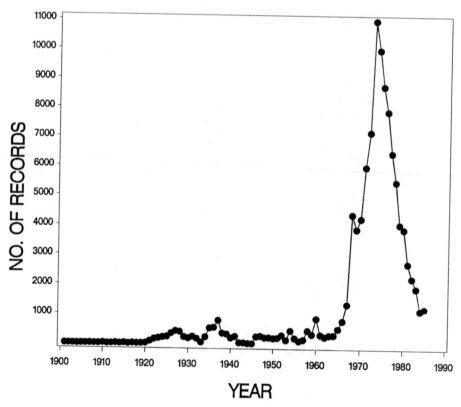

FIG. 1. The number of species records collected by year, 1900–1985.

species were represented by shading. Dots based on specific locality records were used to define range limits. No effort was made to map all non-overlapping locality dots. The Ontario distributions were based on an average of 90 locality records per species in the collection of the Royal Ontario Museum. *The Atlas of North American Freshwater Fishes* (Lee et al., 1980) used these same distribution dots as the primary source for mapping the distributions of 140 Ontario species on a base map of North America.

This study lists 158 species, 5 subspecies, and 2 selected hybrids that are established in, or have been collected in, Ontario. Scientific and common names, and the systematic order of families, follow those given in Robins et al. (1991) and in Appendix 1. Dot distribution maps produced for 141 of these species were based on an average of 700 distribution records per species. These records were derived from the OMNR Fish Species Distribution Data System (FSDDS). This database contains records derived from the OMNR Lake and Stream Inventories, ROM, and NMC. The majority of distribution records in the FSDDS are for the inland waters of Ontario; therefore, there is lack of offshore-distribution data for the Ontario waters of the Great Lakes.

Distribution information and distribution maps for a variety of species occurring in Ontario are also available in status reports of the Committee on the Status of Endangered Wildlife in Canada (COSEWIC) published in *The Canadian Field-Naturalist*. Much of the distribution information for Ontario in those reports was derived from the sources used here.

MATERIALS AND METHODS

Distribution Database

As of January 1987, the FSDDS contained 107,438 records. Each record represents a collection of a single species from a single location on a given date, and contains the following information: waterbody name, latitude, longitude, watershed code (*sensu* Cox, 1978), OMNR species code, date of capture, and source of information. An additional 3,559 ROM records not yet on the FSDDS were added to the distribution database. The OMNR species codes were not used in this publication, but are listed in Dodge et al. (1984), or may be obtained from OMNR Fisheries Policy Branch, Toronto.

Biases inherent in the FSDDS dataset can be characterized by biases recognized in the OMNR Lake Inventory database. Minns (1986) concluded that four game species are overrepresented. A positive correlation between median fork length and number of records was found, suggesting that smaller species (such as cyprinids) are underrepresented (Bowlby and Green, 1987). These trends probably reflect the primary responsibility of the OMNR for economically important (game and commercial) species.

Shortcomings in the FSDDS were identified by comparing species lists for each tertiary watershed, derived from the FSDDS, to lists of species expected to be present in each watershed, derived from the distribution maps of Scott and Crossman (1973a). Some discrepancies are the result of the coarse shading of species ranges in Scott and Crossman (1973a), and some are the result of sampling biases; however, the total lack of records in several tertiary watersheds is the result of absence of sampling. To correct these biases, 4,049 records, including 259 new records for tertiary watersheds, were gathered from OMNR District Offices, the literature, unpublished datasets, and field collections. In total, 7,608 records were added to the FSDDS, raising the number of records contained in this supplemented database to 115,046.

Distribution Maps

After the evaluation of available software packages, SAS/GRAPH (SAS Institute, 1987) was chosen to produce maps of sample sites and species distributions. An unprojected base map of Ontario was downloaded from the University of Toronto mainframe SAS/GRAPH CANADA3 map dataset. This base map was annotated with the southern boundaries of the Great Lakes derived from the PC SAS/GRAPH United States COUNTY map dataset. Nine latitude (45°N, 50°N, and 55°N) and longitude (74°W, 82°W, and 90°W) reference points, designated by crosshairs, were added. Albers' Equal-Area Projection was used to project both the base map and distribution points.

Maps of sampling sites were processed using SAS/GRAPH on the University of Toronto VM/CMS mainframe system and printed on an Apple

LaserWriter postscript laser printer. Sampling sites of all records in the supplemented FSDDS were plotted by latitude and longitude, rounded off to the nearest minute. A map was produced for each of the following periods:
1) prior to 1940—corresponding to the data used by Radforth (1944);
2) 1940–1959—the period preceding increased sampling activity;
3) 1960–1969—ending shortly after the start of the OMNR Lake Inventory; and three periods that represent sampling during the OMNR Lake and Stream Inventories and ending at the last year of records in the FSDDS—two five-year periods, 4) 1970–1974, and 5) 1975–1979; and one six-year period, 6) 1980–1986.

Distribution records for species maps were processed using PC SAS/ GRAPH on an IBM-compatible XT-turbo microcomputer (species with more than 2,000 records were processed on a Compaq 386 microcomputer). Species distribution maps were output on a Hewlett Packard LaserJet Series II printer with 1.5 MB expanded memory. After the maps were produced, any obvious outlier points were checked for error against data at ROM, OMNR, and NMC. If the outlier point was incorrect, the error was corrected in the database, and the map replotted. Errors included incorrect identification of specimens, lack of documentation to substantiate species records, and typing errors. If an outlier point represented a species record with documentation, but was not based on voucher specimens, the record was deemed questionable and excluded from the distribution map.

RESULTS AND DISCUSSION

Fish Fauna

The checklist contains 158 species, 5 subspecies, and 2 hybrids (representing 32 families) that are established or have been collected in Ontario. The list does not contain other forms that are neither common nor readily identifiable. These include hybrids and hybrid backcrosses, dwarf forms, and natural or experimental genetic variants of native species. The list includes only two of many hybrids, simply because they are common and easily distinguishable. These are the splake, a hybrid between the brook trout, *Salvelinus fontinalis,* and the lake trout, *S. namaycush*; and the tiger muskellunge, a hybrid between the northern pike, *Esox lucius,* and the muskellunge, *E. masquinongy.* The tiger muskellunge occurs naturally, whereas splake is present mainly as the result of fish culture. In Ontario, hybridization is also known to occur naturally in other trouts and whitefishes (Salmonidae), minnows (Cyprinidae), suckers (Catostomidae), bullhead catfishes (Ictaluridae), sculpins (Cottidae), and sunfishes (Centrarchidae). The presence of small early-maturing dwarf individuals and larger later-maturing individuals of the same species in single bodies of water has been reported in suckers (Catostomidae) and trouts (Salmonidae). Naturally occurring colour variants have been reported in the northern pike, *Esox lucius,* and the yellow perch, *Perca flavescens.* Several forms of experimentally selected genetic variants of rainbow trout, *Oncorhynchus mykiss,* have been captured in Ontario.

Of the 128 fishes native to Ontario, six are endemic to the Great Lakes and only one, *Salvelinus fontinalis timagamiensis,* is endemic to Ontario. Fifteen species have been designated by COSEWIC as vulnerable (= rare), six as threatened, two as extirpated, one species and one subspecies as extinct, and one subspecies as endangered (Campbell, 1991). The introduction of 55 species into non-native ecosystems has been documented in Ontario. These introduced species (*sensu* Kohler and Courtenay, 1986) can be categorized by vector of introduction. Some species have been introduced by more than one vector. Thirteen species have been intentionally introduced into Ontario, and at least 11 native species are known to have been intentionally transferred between waterbodies within Ontario. Ten species have naturally expanded into Ontario, six have been introduced as the result of release from aquaria, six (including three native species) have been introduced as a result of release from ballast water, and ten (including five native species) have been unintentionally released by various other methods (for further information see status notations in checklist). Of these introductions, 33 have failed, and 19 have established self-reproducing populations; the results of 5 introductions are unknown.

Several species, common and locally abundant elsewhere but not found in

Ontario, are present within 150 km of Ontario. These species may be considered potential invaders (Table 3). Three species present in Ontario are also listed in Table 3, since dispersal through the suggested routes would lead to significant range extensions in Ontario. Some of the species in Table 3 have northern range limits along the boundary waters of the Great Lakes, and some have recently extended their ranges towards Ontario (e.g., *Notropis texanus*). The addition of introduced species often results in deleterious consequences. Therefore, it is important for all individuals working in aquatic environments on probable invasion routes to closely examine fish collections for the presence of invaders.

Distribution of Sampling Sites, 1900–1986

The earliest records in the FSDDS are dated around 1900; therefore, in the 40 years prior to 1940, our knowledge of the fauna was based on 6,000 records collected from 2,299 sites. Southern Ontario outside of the Algonquin Uplands was widely sampled, most intensively in southeastern Ontario by the ROM (e.g., Toner, 1937; Dymond, 1939). Northern Ontario had been sparsely sampled except for Lake Nipigon and Lake Abitibi, which were well sampled by the Ontario Fisheries Research Laboratory of the University of Toronto in the 1920s (Dymond, 1926; Dymond and Hart, 1927; see Fig. 2). Largely as the result of World War II, fewer records (4,760 records at 1,933 sites) were obtained between 1940 and 1959. Southern Ontario, including the Algonquin Uplands, was widely but not intensively sampled during this period. Except for Lake Abitibi and the north shore of Lake Superior, northern Ontario was sparsely sampled (Fig. 2).

Sampling increased dramatically between 1960 and 1969 (12,121 records at 3,055 sites), reflecting the continuing work of the ROM and an increase in sampling resulting from the initiation of the OMNR Lake Inventory. Southern Ontario was widely and more extensively sampled. Northern Ontario was broadly sampled to the south of 51° north latitude, and sparsely to the north of it (Fig. 2). The period between 1970 and 1974 has been the most intensively sampled to date (47,159 records at 11,627 sites), as the result of the advent of the OMNR Stream Inventory in 1971. Southern Ontario was thoroughly sampled except for Essex County, which contains few streams. Northern Ontario was well sampled south of 52° north latitude, and more sparsely to the north of it (Fig. 2). Although less intensively sampled between 1975 and 1979 (27,954 records at 5,039 sites), most of Ontario was widely sampled, except for the Hudson Bay Lowlands (Fig. 2). A drastic decrease in sampling (9,314 records at 1,423 sites) occurred between 1980 and 1986. Only southcentral Ontario and northwestern Ontario south of 52° north latitude show any degree of sampling intensity during this period (Fig. 2).

In general, southern Ontario has been widely and well sampled. Widespread sampling has taken place in northern Ontario, south of 52° north latitude. There are several large areas immediately south of this parallel, and several

9

TABLE 3. Potential fish invaders of Ontario.

Scientific Name	Common Name	Probable Invasion Route	Nearest Population (Distance)[1]
Esox americanus americanus	redfin pickerel	St. Lawrence River	Lac St. Pierre, PQ (125)
Esox niger	chain pickerel	St. Lawrence River	Indian River, NY (50)
Exoglossum laurae	tonguetied minnow	Lake Ontario	Genessee River, NY (80)
Notropis amblops	bigeye chub	Niagara River	E tribs. of Lake Ontario, NY (15)
Semotilus corporalis[2]	fallfish	Niagara River	Tonawanda Creek, NY (30)
Lepomis megalotis[2]	longear sunfish	Niagara River	Tonawanda Creek, NY (30)
Notropis dorsalis	bigmouth shiner	Niagara River	Buffalo Creek, NY (10)
Notropis amblops	bigeye chub	Lake Erie	SW tribs. of Lake Erie, OH (80)
Notropis buccatus	silverjaw minnow	Lake Erie	W tribs. of Lake Erie, MI (25)
Phenacobius mirabilis	suckermouth minnow	Lake Erie	W tribs. of Lake Erie, OH (100)
Phoxinus erythrogaster	southern redbelly dace	Lake Erie	W tribs. of Lake Erie, MI (75)
Lepomis microlophus	redear sunfish	Lake Erie	SW tribs. of Lake Erie, OH (80)
Etheostoma variatum	variegate darter	Lake Erie	S tribs. of Lake Erie, NY (125)
Etheostoma zonale	banded darter	Lake Erie	S tribs. of Lake Erie, NY (125)
Etheostoma spectabile	orangethroat darter	Detroit River	W tribs. of Detroit River, MI (1)
Proterorhinus marmoratus	tubenose goby	St. Clair River	W shore of St. Clair River, MI (0.5)
Morone americana[2]	white perch	Lake Superior	U.S. waters
Notropis blennius	river shiner	Rainy River	S tribs. of Rainy River, MN (5)
		Lake of the Woods	Lake of the Woods, MN (5)
Notropis texanus	weed shiner	Winnipeg River	near Great Falls, MB (125)

1   Distance (water distance in kilometres) of population nearest to Ontario
2   Present in other parts of Ontario

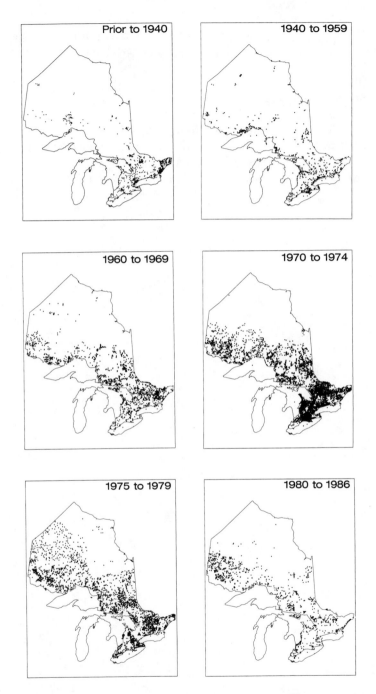

FIG. 2. History of effort put into sampling the freshwater fish fauna of Ontario 1900–1986. Number of stations is not cumulative over the series.

small isolated areas throughout northern Ontario, that have not been sampled. Little is known of the faunas of the Hudson Bay and James Bay tributaries to the north of this parallel.

Species Distribution Maps

One hundred and forty-one species distribution maps are presented here. These maps are presented in the same order as the species in the checklist. Maps are not provided for the two hybrids and for twenty-two introduced species that have failed to become established in Ontario waters.

CHECKLIST OF ONTARIO FRESHWATER FISHES

The systematic order of families and names of species reflects that accepted by the Joint Names Committee of the American Fisheries Society and American Society of Ichthyologists and Herpetologists, and published in *A List of Common and Scientific Names of Fishes from the United States and Canada* (Robins et al., 1991). Note that the systematic order of families and some names of species have changed since Robins et al. (1980). See Appendix 1 for a list of the changes in scientific names. The status column provides information on the origin or nature of the populations in Ontario (e.g., native, introduced, etc.). The symbol * identifies the 2 hybrids and 22 failed introductions for which there are no distribution maps.

Key to Status Codes

E—Endemic: A naturally occurring species that is restricted in its global distribution to the Great Lakes or Ontario

N—Native: A naturally occurring species that is not restricted to Ontario

I(x,y)—Introduced: A species intentionally or unintentionally introduced into non-native ecosystems

  x = 1 Intentional introduction
  x = 2 Intentional transfer of native species between basins
  x = 3 Unintentional introduction by ship ballast water
  x = 4 Unintentional introduction by aquarium release
  x = 5 Natural dispersal into Ontario
  x = 6 Unintentional introduction by various methods
  y = S Successful; self-reproducing population(s) established
  y = F Failed; self-reproducing population(s) not established
  y = U Unknown; not known if self-reproducing population(s) established

V—Vulnerable (= Rare): A species or subspecies at risk due to low or declining numbers, or due to occurrence at the fringe of its range or in restricted areas

T—Threatened: A species or subspecies likely to become endangered in Ontario if factors affecting its vulnerability are not reversed

EN—Endangered: A species or subspecies threatened with imminent extirpation or extinction in Ontario

EX—Extirpated: A formerly native species or subspecies, no longer occurring in Ontario, but still occurring elsewhere

X—Extinct: A formerly native species or subspecies, no longer occurring in Ontario or anywhere else in the world

Scientific Name	Common Name	Status
PETROMYZONTIDAE	**Lampreys**	
Ichthyomyzon fossor	northern brook lamprey	N
Ichthyomyzon unicuspis	silver lamprey	N
Lampetra appendix	American brook lamprey	N
Petromyzon marinus	sea lamprey	I(6,S)
ACIPENSERIDAE	**Sturgeons**	
Acipenser fulvescens	lake sturgeon	N
POLYODONTIDAE	**Paddlefishes**	
Polyodon spathula	paddlefish	N, EX
LEPISOSTEIDAE	**Gars**	
Lepisosteus oculatus	spotted gar	N, V
Lepisosteus osseus	longnose gar	N
*Lepisosteus platyrhyncus**	Florida gar	I(4,F)
AMIIDAE	**Bowfins**	
Amia calva	bowfin	N, I(6,F)
HIODONTIDAE	**Mooneyes**	
Hiodon alosoides	goldeye	N
Hiodon tergisus	mooneye	N
ANGUILLIDAE	**Freshwater Eels**	
Anguilla rostrata	American eel	N, I(3,F)
CLUPEIDAE	**Herrings**	
Alosa pseudoharengus	alewife	I(6,S)
Alosa sapidissima	American shad	N, I(2,F)
Dorosoma cepedianum	gizzard shad	N
CYPRINIDAE	**Carps and Minnows**	
Campostoma anomalum	central stoneroller	N, I(6,F), V
Carassius auratus	goldfish	I(6,S)
Clinostomus elongatus	redside dace	N, V
Couesius plumbeus	lake chub	N
*Ctenopharyngodon idella**	grass carp	I(5,F)
Cyprinella spiloptera	spotfin shiner	N

*Distribution map not provided.
E—Endemic; I—Introduced; N—Native.
EN—Endangered; EX—Extirpated; T—Threatened; V—Vulnerable; X—Extinct.

Scientific Name	Common Name	Status
Cyprinus carpio	common carp	I(1,S)
Erimystax x-punctatus	gravel chub	N, EX
Exoglossum maxillingua	cutlips minnow	N
Hybognathus hankinsoni	brassy minnow	N
Hybognathus regius	eastern silvery minnow	N
Luxilus chrysocephalus	striped shiner	N
Luxilus cornutus	common shiner	N
Lythrurus umbratilis	redfin shiner	N
Macrhybopsis storeriana	silver chub	N, V
Margariscus margarita	pearl dace	N
Nocomis biguttatus	hornyhead chub	N, I(6,F)
Nocomis micropogon	river chub	N, I(6,F)
Notemigonus crysoleucas	golden shiner	N
Notropis anogenus	pugnose shiner	N, V
Notropis atherinoides	emerald shiner	N
Notropis bifrenatus	bridle shiner	N
Notropis buchanani	ghost shiner	I(5,S)
Notropis heterodon	blackchin shiner	N
Notropis heterolepis	blacknose shiner	N
Notropis hudsonius	spottail shiner	N
Notropis photogenis	silver shiner	N, V
Notropis rubellus	rosyface shiner	N
Notropis stramineus	sand shiner	N
Notropis volucellus	mimic shiner	N
Opsopoeodus emiliae	pugnose minnow	N, V
Phoxinus eos	northern redbelly dace	N
Phoxinus neogaeus	finescale dace	N
Pimephales notatus	bluntnose minnow	N
Pimephales promelas	fathead minnow	N
Rhinichthys atratulus	blacknose dace	N
Rhinichthys cataractae	longnose dace	N
Scardinius erythrophthalmus*	rudd	I(6,U)
Semotilus atromaculatus	creek chub	N
Semotilus corporalis	fallfish	N
CATOSTOMIDAE	**Suckers**	
Carpiodes cyprinus	quillback	N
Catostomus catostomus	longnose sucker	N

I(x,y): x=1, Intentionally introduced; x=2, Transfer of native species; x=3, Ballast water; x=4, Aquarium release; x=5, Natural dispersal; x=6, Various methods; y=S, Successful; y=F, Failed; y=U, Unknown.

Scientific Name	Common Name	Status
Catostomus commersoni	white sucker	N
Erimyzon sucetta	lake chubsucker	N
Hypentelium nigricans	northern hognose sucker	N
Ictiobus cyprinellus*	bigmouth buffalo	I(5,F), V
Ictiobus niger*	black buffalo	I(5,F), V
Minytrema melanops	spotted sucker	N, V
Moxostoma anisurum	silver redhorse	N
Moxostoma carinatum	river redhorse	N, V
Moxostoma duquesnei	black redhorse	N, T
Moxostoma erythrurum	golden redhorse	N
Moxostoma macrolepidotum	shorthead redhorse	N
Moxostoma valenciennesi	greater redhorse	N

CHARACIDAE — **Characins**

Colossoma bidens*	pacu	I(4,F)

ICTALURIDAE — **Bullhead Catfishes**

Ameiurus melas	black bullhead	N
Ameiurus natalis	yellow bullhead	N
Ameiurus nebulosus	brown bullhead	N
Ictalurus punctatus	channel catfish	N
Noturus flavus	stonecat	N
Noturus gyrinus	tadpole madtom	N
Noturus insignis*	margined madtom	I(6,F), T
Noturus miurus	brindled madtom	N, V
Noturus stigmosus*	northern madtom	I(5,F)
Pylodictis olivaris*	flathead catfish	I(5,F)

LORICARIIDAE — **Suckermouth Catfishes**

Panaque nigrolineatus*	royal panaque	I(4,F)

ESOCIDAE — **Pikes**

Esox americanus vermiculatus	grass pickerel	N
Esox lucius	northern pike	N
Esox lucius X *Esox masquinongy**	tiger muskellunge	N
Esox masquinongy	muskellunge	N, I(2,S)

*Distribution map not provided.
E—Endemic; I—Introduced; N—Native.
EN—Endangered; EX—Extirpated; T—Threatened; V—Vulnerable; X—Extinct.

Scientific Name	Common Name	Status
UMBRIDAE	**Mudminnows**	
*Dallia pectoralis**	Alaska blackfish	I(1,F)
Umbra limi	central mudminnow	N
OSMERIDAE	**Smelts**	
Osmerus mordax	rainbow smelt	N, I(6,S)
SALMONIDAE	**Trouts**	
Coregonus artedi	cisco or lake herring	N, I(2,S)
Coregonus clupeaformis	lake whitefish	N
Coregonus hoyi	bloater	E
Coregonus johannae	deepwater cisco	E, X
Coregonus kiyi	kiyi	E, V
Coregonus nigripinnis	blackfin cisco	E, T
Coregonus reighardi	shortnose cisco	E, T
Coregonus zenithicus	shortjaw cisco	N, T
Oncorhynchus gorbuscha	pink salmon	I(1,S)
*Oncorhynchus keta**	chum salmon	I(1,F)
Oncorhynchus kisutch	coho salmon	I(1,S)
*Oncorhynchus masou**	cherry salmon	I(1,F)
Oncorhynchus mykiss	rainbow trout	I(1,S)
*Oncorhynchus nerka**	sockeye salmon	I(1,F)
Oncorhynchus tshawytscha	chinook salmon	I(1,S)
Prosopium coulteri	pygmy whitefish	N
Prosopium cylindraceum	round whitefish	N
Salmo salar	Atlantic salmon	N, I(1,U)
Salmo trutta	brown trout	I(1,S)
Salvelinus alpinus	Arctic char	N, I(1,F)
Salvelinus fontinalis fontinalis	brook trout	N, I(2,S,F)
Salvelinus fontinalis timagamiensis (after Qadri, 1968)	Aurora trout	E, I(2,U), EN
Salvelinus fontinalis X *Salvelinus namaycush**	splake	I(1,F)
Salvelinus namaycush	lake trout	N, I(2,S,F)
*Thymallus arcticus**	Arctic grayling	I(1,F)

I(x,y): x=1, Intentionally introduced; x=2, Transfer of native species; x=3, Ballast water; x=4, Aquarium release; x=5, Natural dispersal; x=6, Various methods; y=S, Successful; y=F, Failed; y=U, Unknown.

Scientific Name	Common Name	Status
PERCOPSIDAE	**Trout-perches**	
Percopsis omiscomaycus	trout-perch	N
GADIDAE	**Codfishes**	
Lota lota	burbot	N
CYPRINODONTIDAE	**Killifishes**	
Fundulus diaphanus	banded killifish	N
Fundulus notatus	blackstripe topminnow	N, V
POECILIIDAE	**Livebearers**	
*Gambusia affinis**	mosquitofish	I(4,F)
ATHERINIDAE	**Silversides**	
Labidesthes sicculus	brook silverside	N
GASTEROSTEIDAE	**Sticklebacks**	
Apeltes quadracus	fourspine stickleback	I(3,S)
Culaea inconstans	brook stickleback	N
Gasterosteus aculeatus	threespine stickleback	N, I(3,S)
Pungitius pungitius	ninespine stickleback	N
COTTIDAE	**Sculpins**	
Cottus bairdi	mottled sculpin	N
Cottus cognatus	slimy sculpin	N
Cottus ricei	spoonhead sculpin	N
Myoxocephalus quadricornis	fourhorn sculpin	N
Myoxocephalus thompsoni	deepwater sculpin	N, T
CYCLOPTERIDAE	**Snailfishes**	
*Cyclopterus lumpus**	lumpfish	I(5,F)
PERCICHTHYIDAE	**Temperate Basses**	
Morone americana	white perch	I(5,S)
Morone chrysops	white bass	N
CENTRARCHIDAE	**Sunfishes**	
Ambloplites rupestris	rock bass	N
Lepomis cyanellus	green sunfish	N

*Distribution map not provided.
E—Endemic; I—Introduced; N—Native.
EN—Endangered; EX—Extirpated; T—Threatened; V—Vulnerable; X—Extinct.

Scientific Name	Common Name	Status
Lepomis gibbosus	pumpkinseed	N
Lepomis gulosus	warmouth	I(5,S)
Lepomis humilis	orangespotted sunfish	I(5,S), V
Lepomis macrochirus	bluegill	N
Lepomis megalotis	longear sunfish	N
Micropterus dolomieu	smallmouth bass	N, I(2,S)
Micropterus salmoides	largemouth bass	N, I(2,S)
Pomoxis annularis	white crappie	N
Pomoxis nigromaculatus	black crappie	N
PERCIDAE	**Perches**	
Ammocrypta pellucida	eastern sand darter	N
Etheostoma blennioides	greenside darter	N
Etheostoma caeruleum	rainbow darter	N
Etheostoma exile	Iowa darter	N
Etheostoma flabellare	fantail darter	N
Etheostoma microperca	least darter	N
Etheostoma nigrum	johnny darter	N
Etheostoma olmstedi	tessellated darter	N
Gymnocephalus cernuus*	ruffe	I(3,U)
Perca flavescens	yellow perch	N
Percina caprodes	logperch	N
Percina copelandi	channel darter	N
Percina maculata	blackside darter	N
Percina shumardi	river darter	N
Stizostedion canadense	sauger	N
Stizostedion vitreum glaucum	blue pike	E, X
Stizostedion vitreum vitreum	walleye	N, I(2,S)
SCIAENIDAE	**Drums**	
Aplodinotus grunniens	freshwater drum	N
CICHLIDAE	**Cichlids**	
Astronotus ocellatus*	oscar	I(4,F)
Cichlosoma managuense*	jaguar guapote	I(4,F)
GOBIIDAE	**Gobies**	
Neogobius melanostomus*	round goby	I(3,U)
(after Miller, 1986)		

I(x,y): x=1, Intentionally introduced; x=2, Transfer of native species; x=3, Ballast water; x=4, Aquarium release; x=5, Natural dispersal; x=6, Various methods; y=S, Successful; y=F, Failed; y=U, Unknown.

Scientific Name	Common Name	Status
PLEURONECTIDAE	**Righteye Flounders**	
*Platichthys flesus**	European flounder	I(3,F)

* Distribution map not provided.
E—Endemic; I—Introduced; N—Native.
EN—Endangered; EX—Extirpated; T—Threatened; V—Vulnerable; X—Extinct.

I(x,y): x=1, Intentionally introduced; x=2, Transfer of native species; x=3, Ballast water; x=4, Aquarium release; x=5, Natural dispersal; x=6, Various methods; y=S, Successful; y=F, Failed; y=U, Unknown.

DISTRIBUTION MAPS OF
ONTARIO FRESHWATER FISHES

Ichthyomyzon fossor
northern brook lamprey

Ichthyomyzon unicuspis
silver lamprey

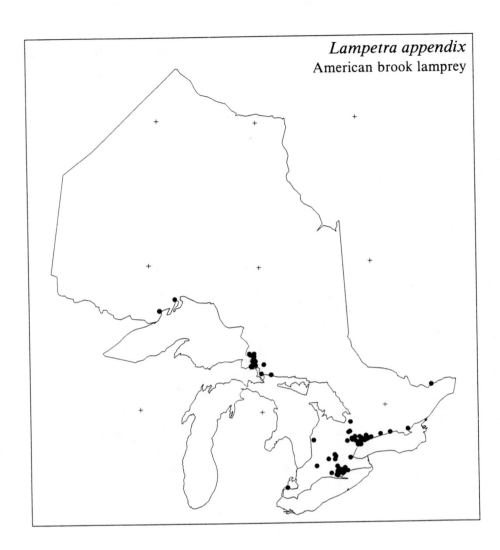

Lampetra appendix
American brook lamprey

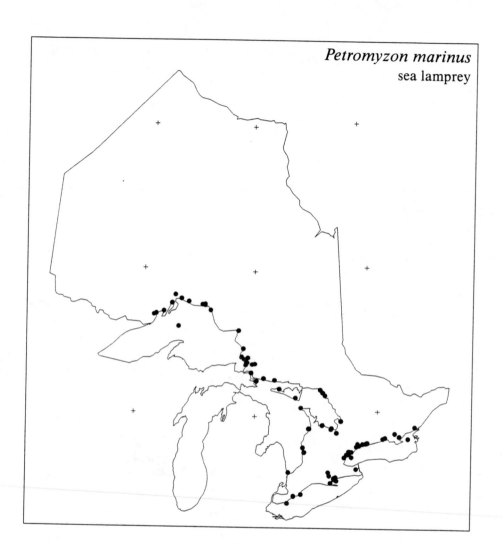

Petromyzon marinus
sea lamprey

Acipenser fulvescens
lake sturgeon

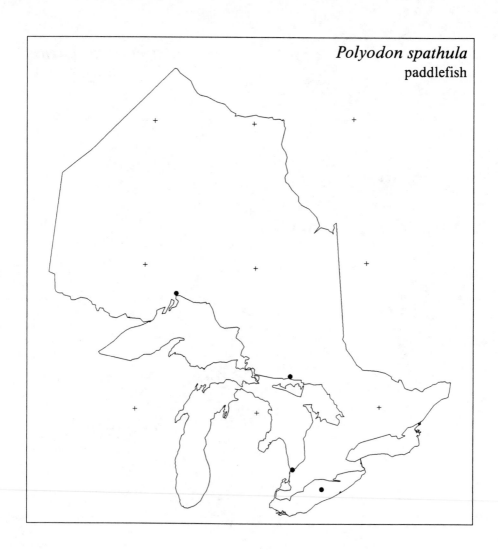

Polyodon spathula
paddlefish

Lepisosteus oculatus
spotted gar

27

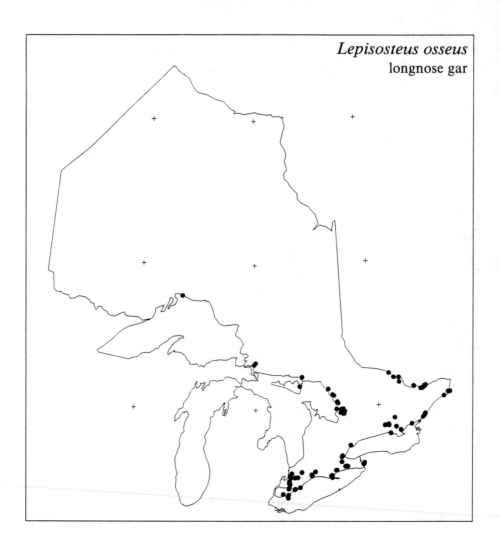

Lepisosteus osseus
longnose gar

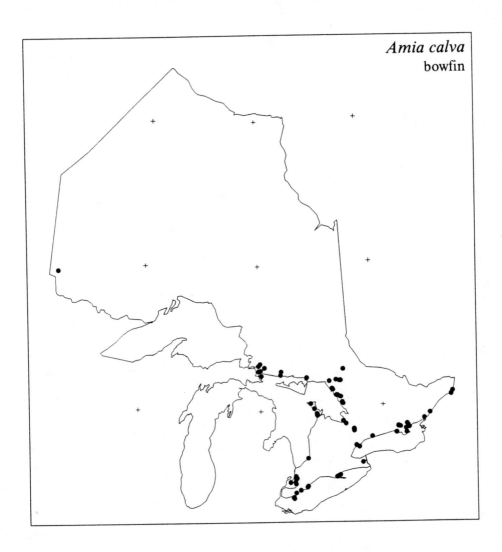

Amia calva
bowfin

Hiodon alosoides
goldeye

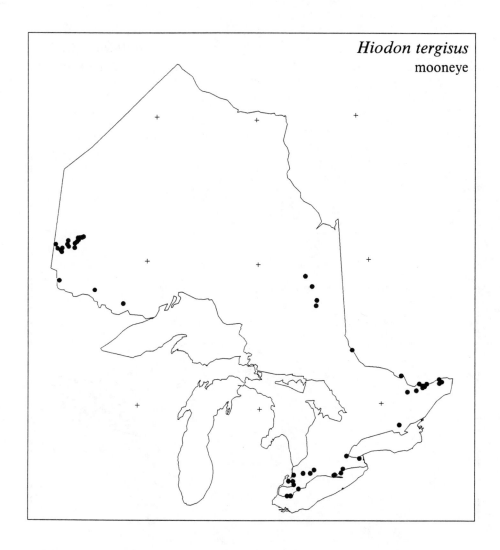

Hiodon tergisus
mooneye

31

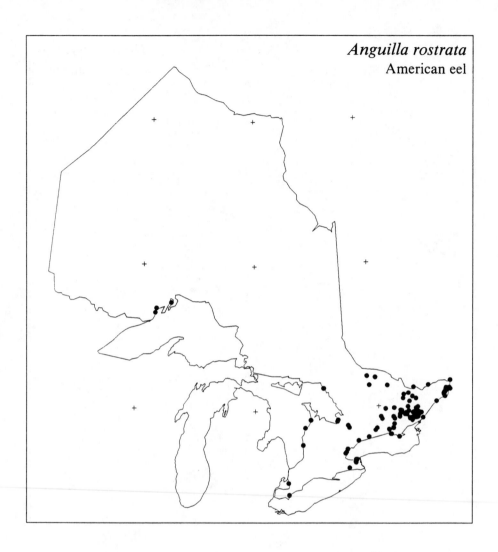

Anguilla rostrata
American eel

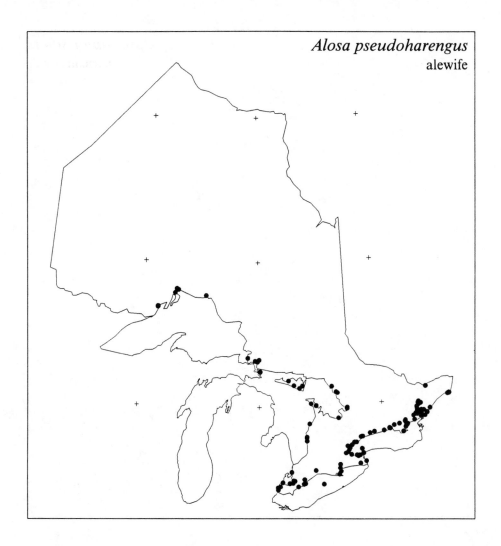

Alosa pseudoharengus
alewife

Alosa sapidissima
American shad

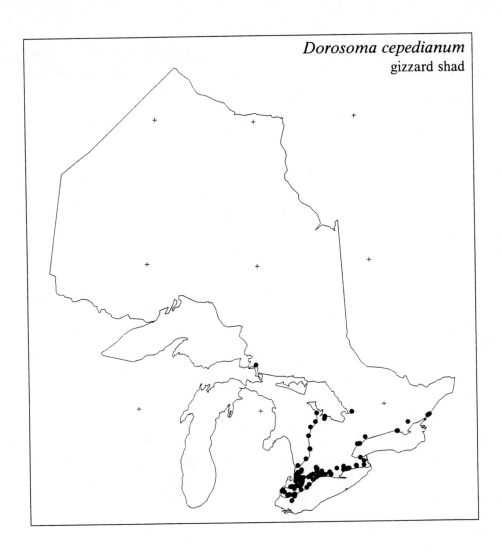

Dorosoma cepedianum
gizzard shad

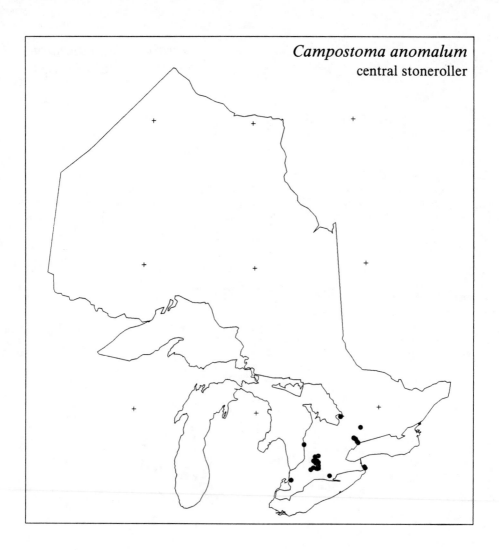

Campostoma anomalum
central stoneroller

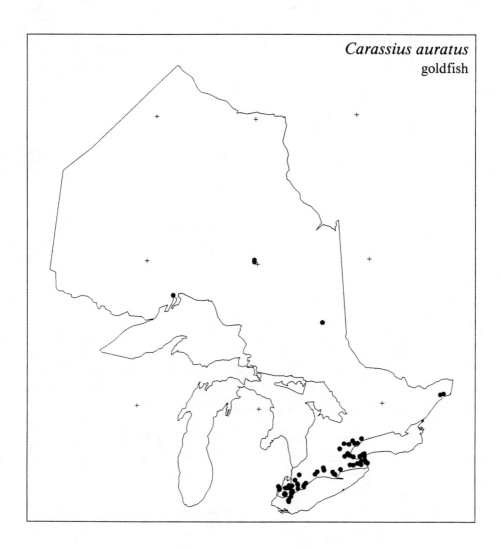

Carassius auratus
goldfish

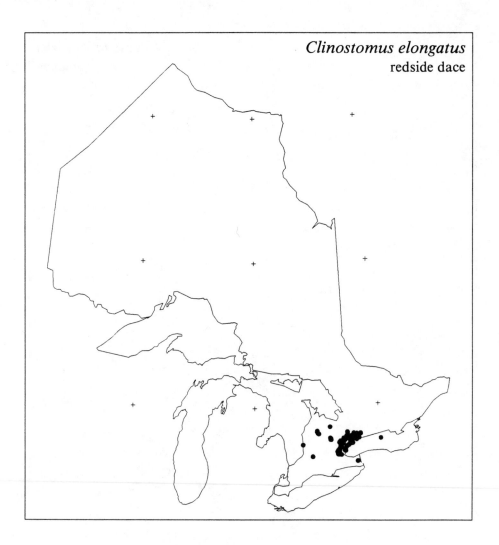

Clinostomus elongatus
redside dace

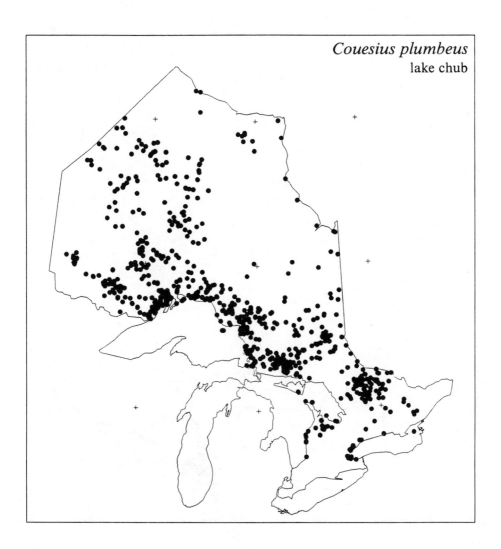

Couesius plumbeus
lake chub

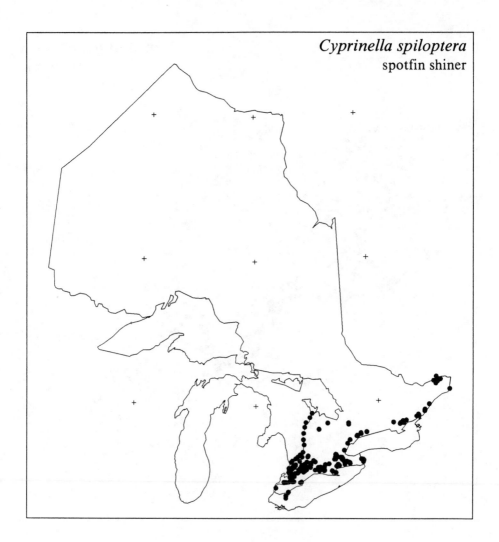

Cyprinella spiloptera
spotfin shiner

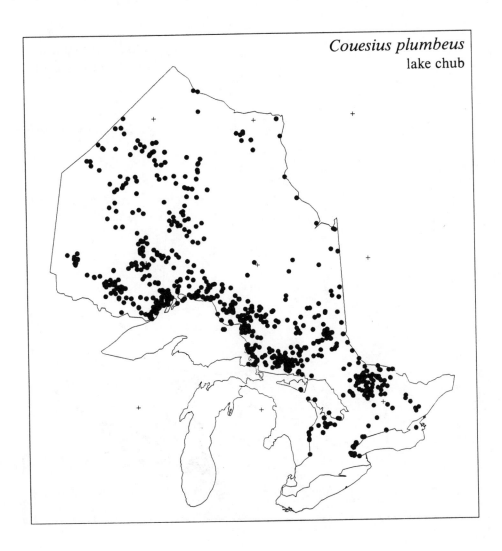

Couesius plumbeus
lake chub

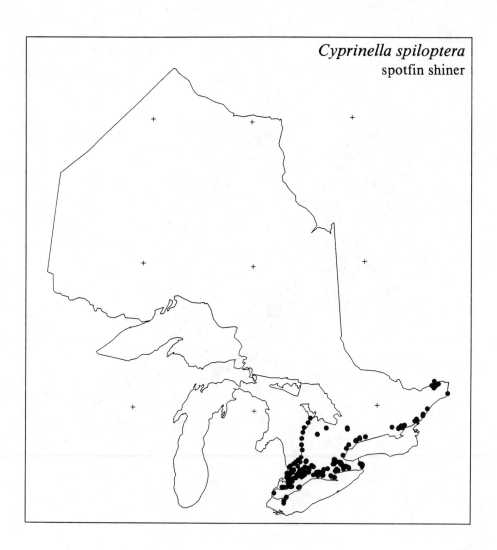

Cyprinella spiloptera
spotfin shiner

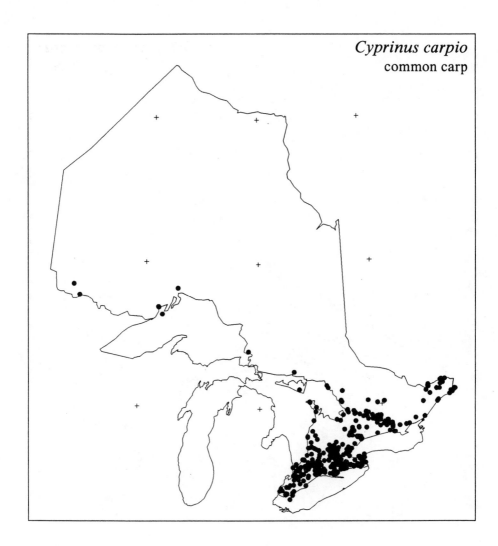

Cyprinus carpio
common carp

Erimystax x-punctatus
gravel chub

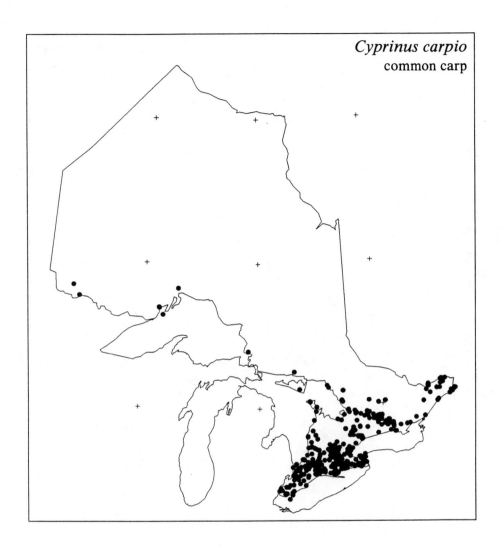

Cyprinus carpio
common carp

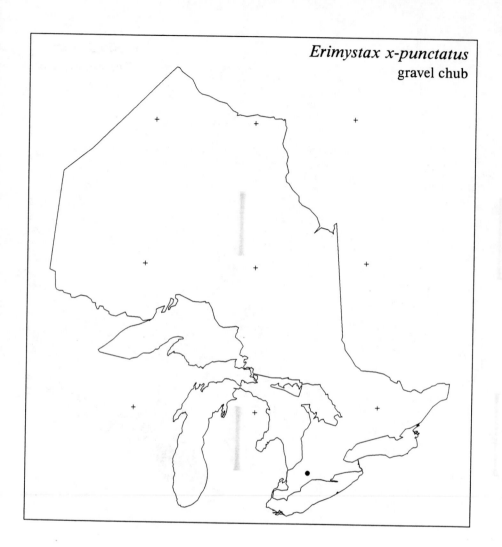

Erimystax x-punctatus
gravel chub

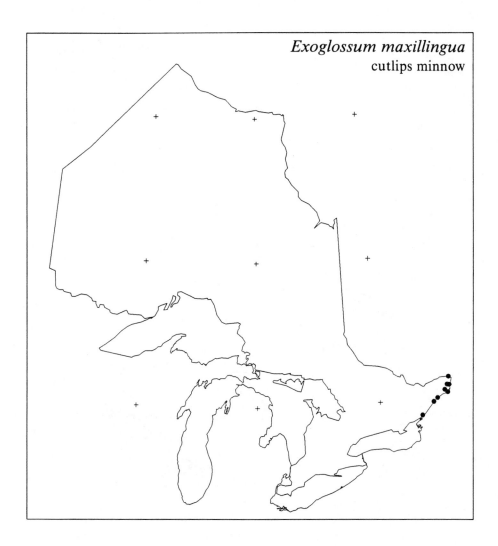

Exoglossum maxillingua
cutlips minnow

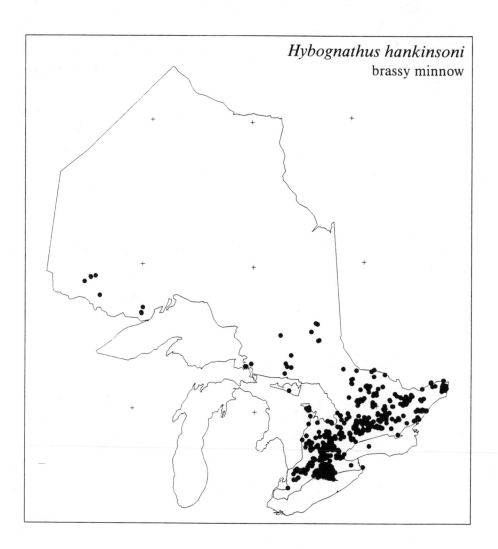

Hybognathus hankinsoni
brassy minnow

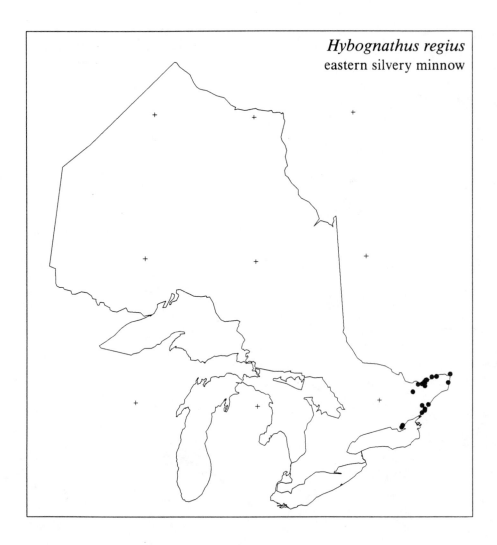

Hybognathus regius
eastern silvery minnow

45

Luxilus chrysocephalus
striped shiner

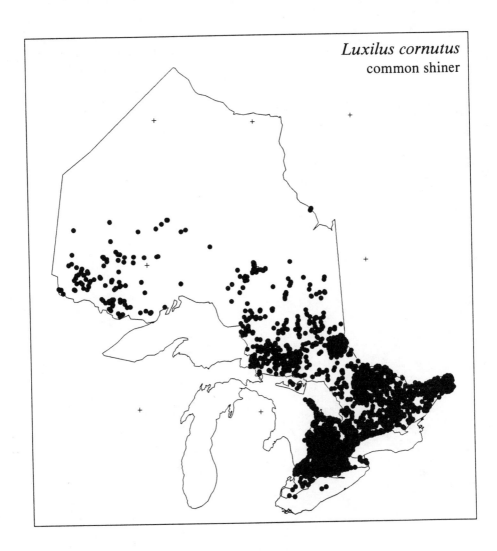

Luxilus cornutus
common shiner

47

Lythrurus umbratilis
redfin shiner

Macrhybopsis storeriana
silver chub

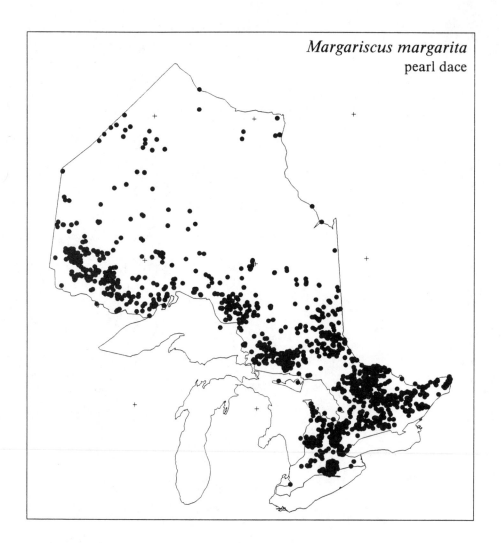

Margariscus margarita
pearl dace

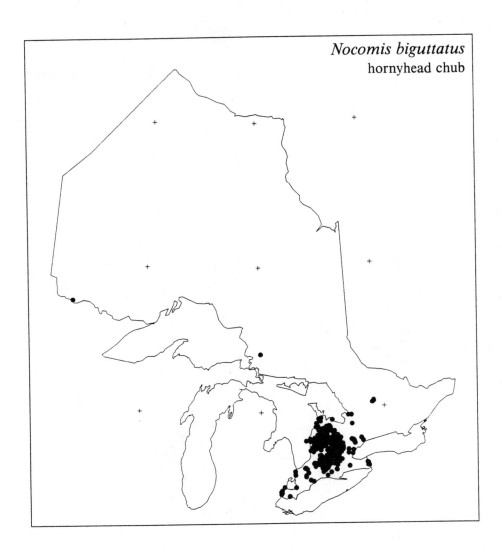

Nocomis biguttatus
hornyhead chub

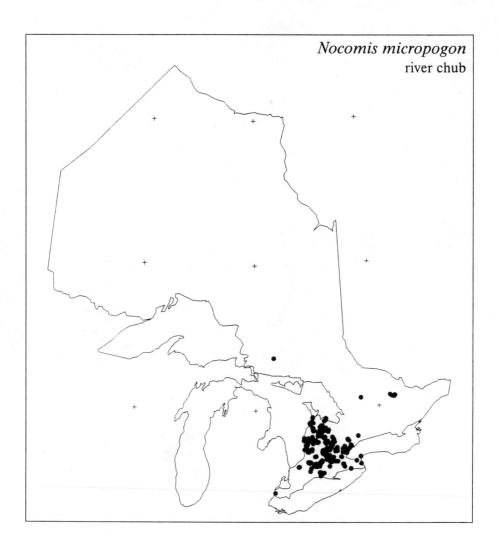

Nocomis micropogon
river chub

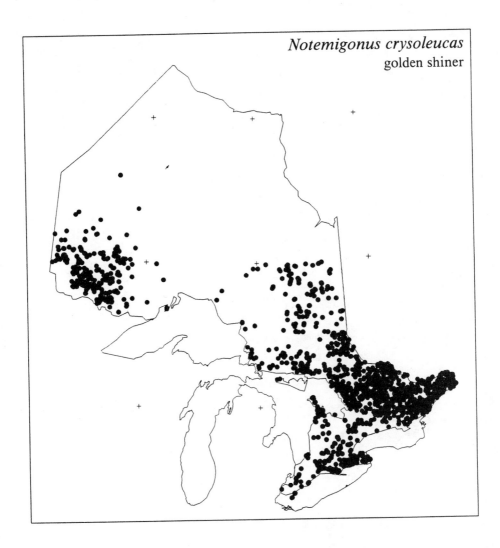

Notemigonus crysoleucas
golden shiner

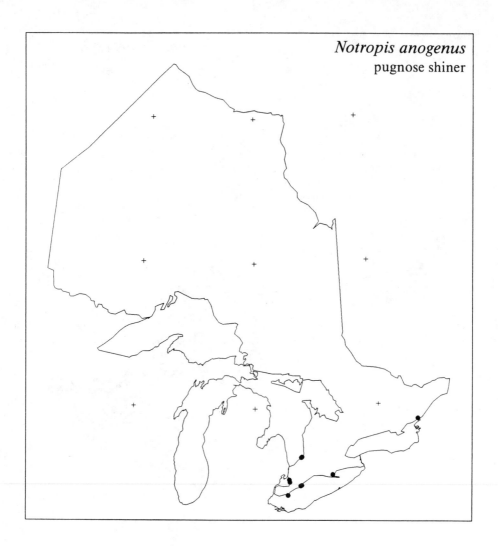

Notropis anogenus
pugnose shiner

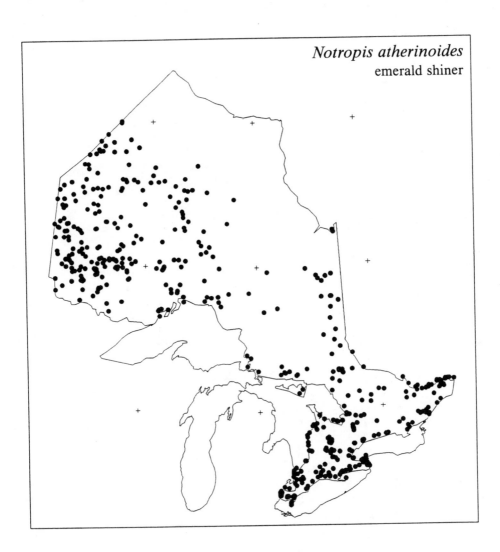

Notropis atherinoides
emerald shiner

55

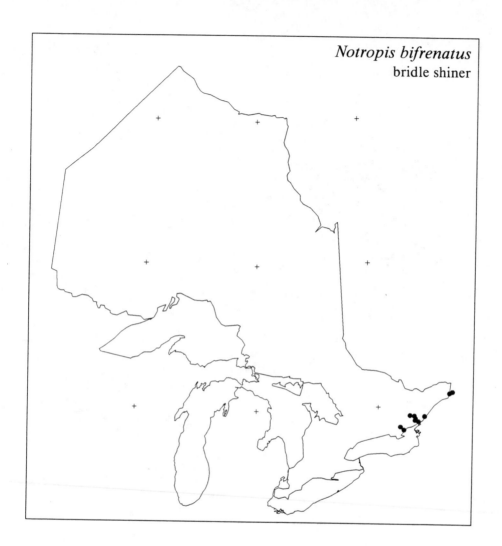

Notropis bifrenatus
bridle shiner

Notropis buchanani
ghost shiner

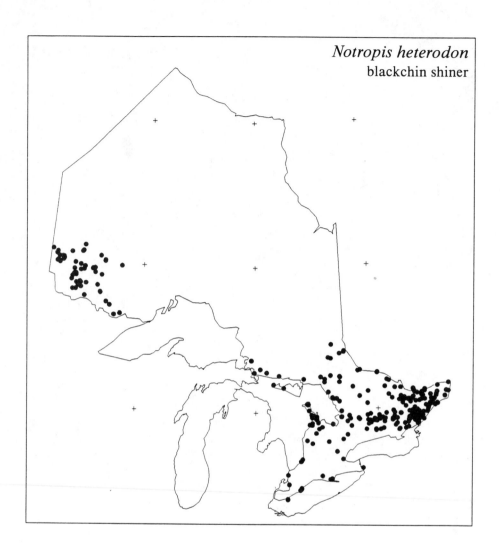

Notropis heterodon
blackchin shiner

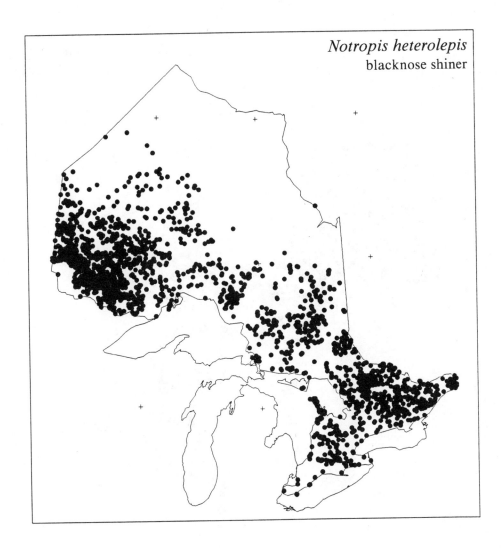

Notropis heterolepis
blacknose shiner

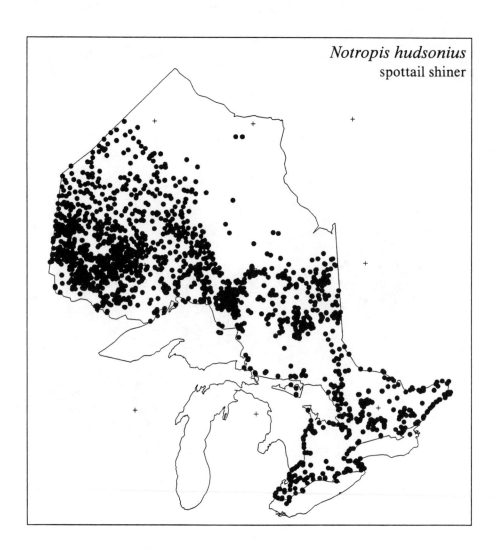

Notropis hudsonius
spottail shiner

Notropis photogenis
silver shiner

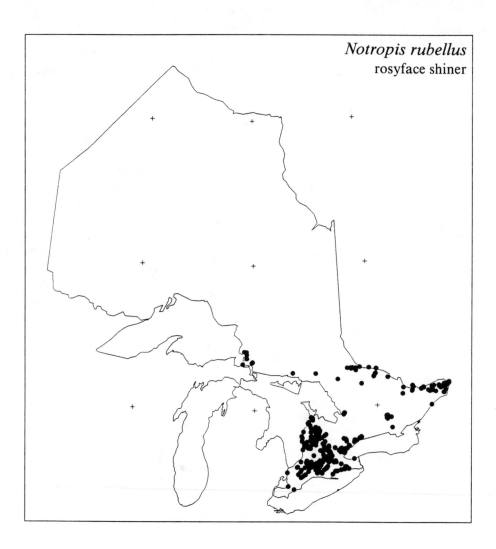

Notropis rubellus
rosyface shiner

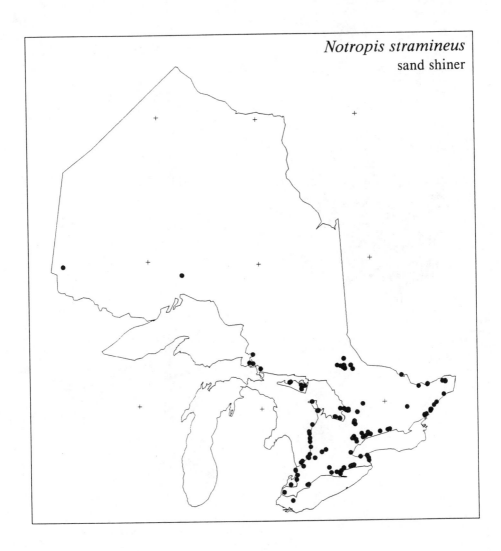

Notropis stramineus
sand shiner

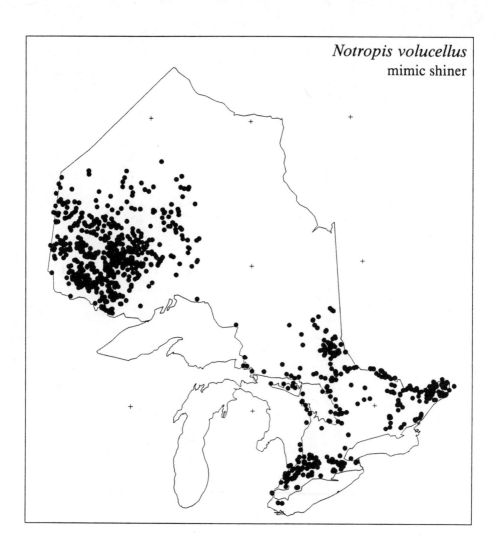

Notropis volucellus
mimic shiner

Opsopoeodus emiliae
pugnose minnow

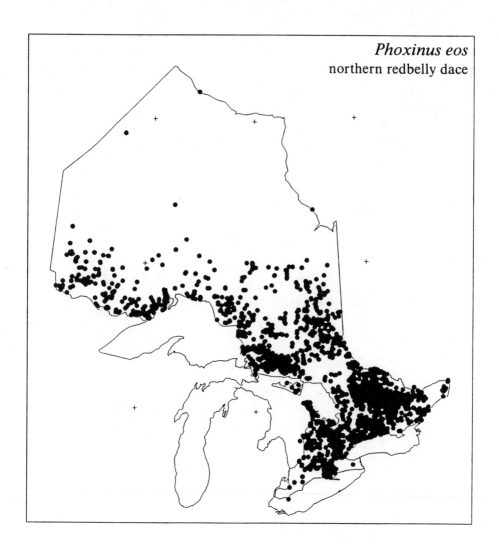

Phoxinus eos
northern redbelly dace

66

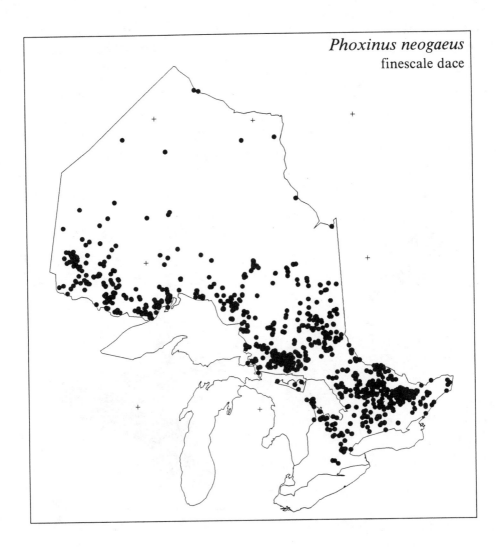

Phoxinus neogaeus
finescale dace

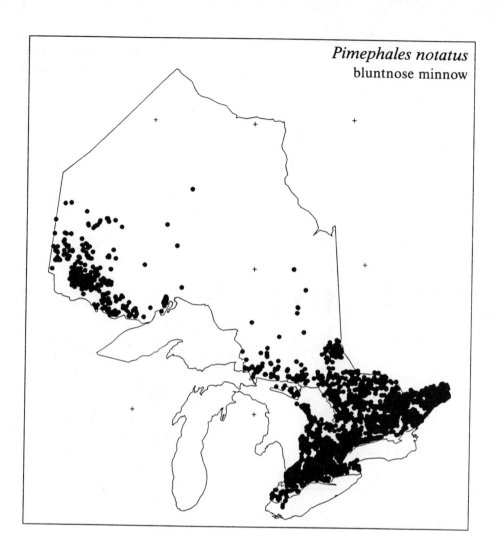

Pimephales notatus
bluntnose minnow

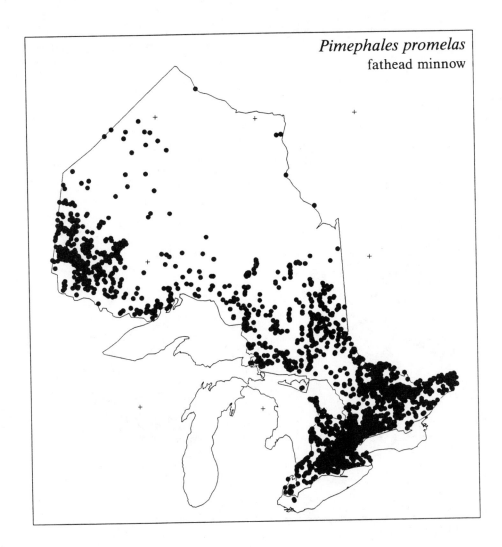

Pimephales promelas
fathead minnow

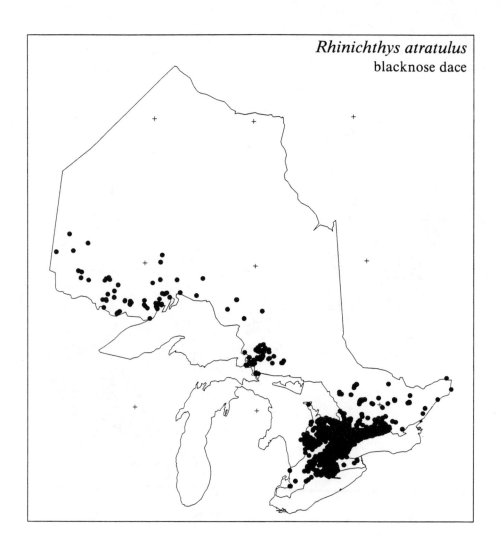

Rhinichthys atratulus
blacknose dace

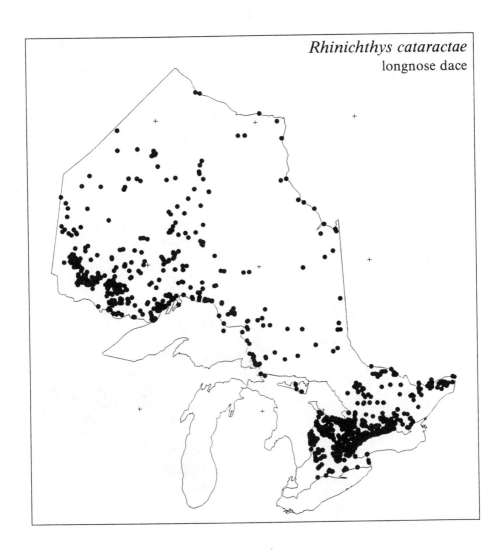

Rhinichthys cataractae
longnose dace

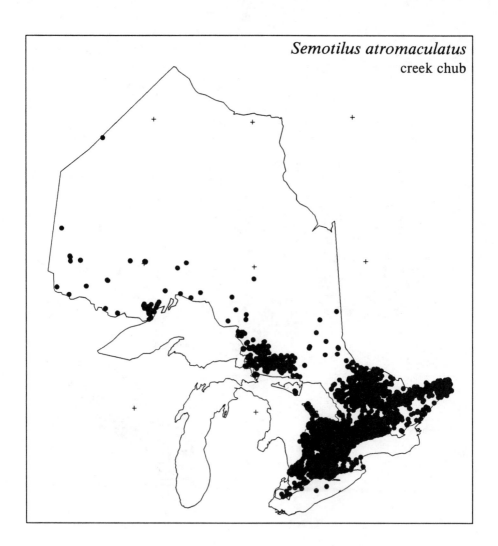

Semotilus atromaculatus
creek chub

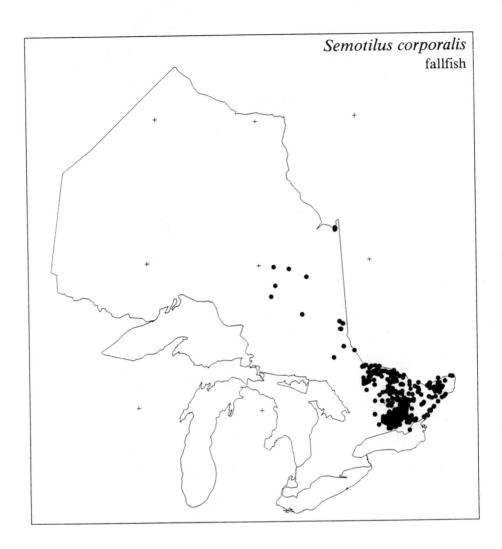

Semotilus corporalis
fallfish

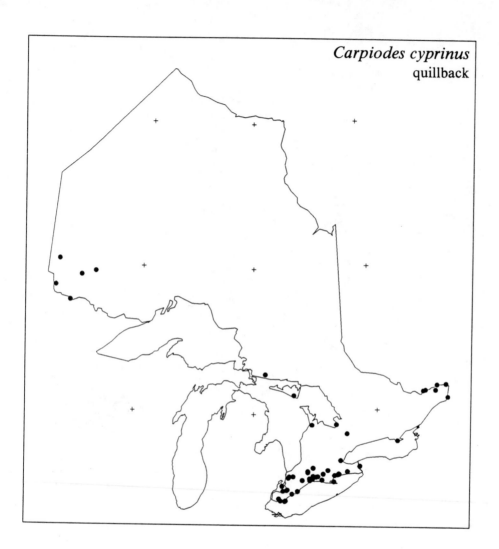

Carpiodes cyprinus
quillback

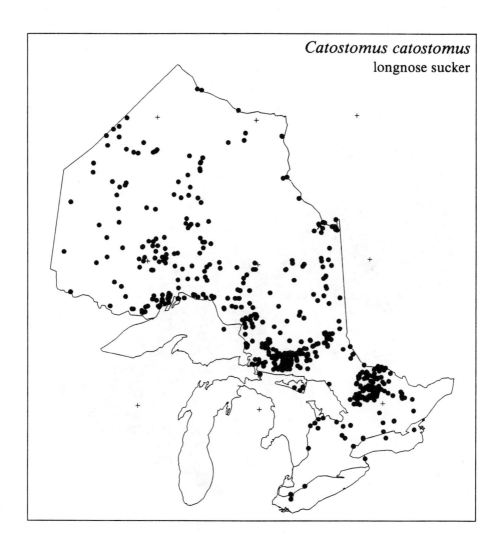

Catostomus catostomus
longnose sucker

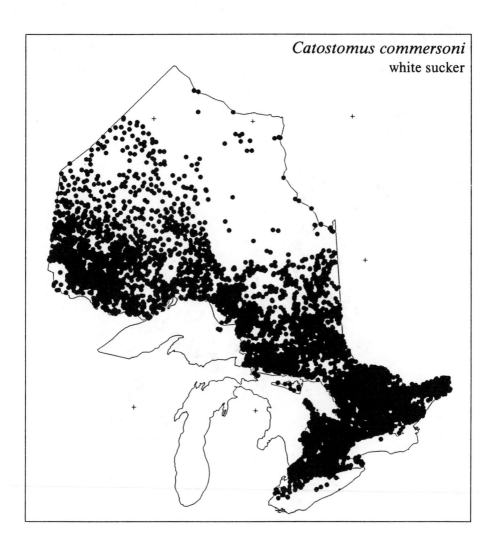

Catostomus commersoni
white sucker

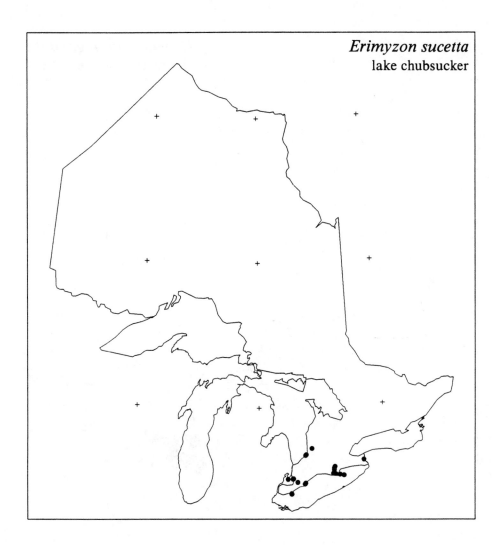

Erimyzon sucetta
lake chubsucker

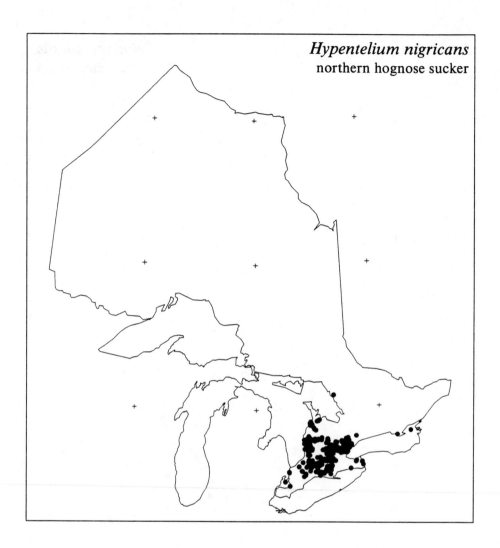

Hypentelium nigricans
northern hognose sucker

Minytrema melanops
spotted sucker

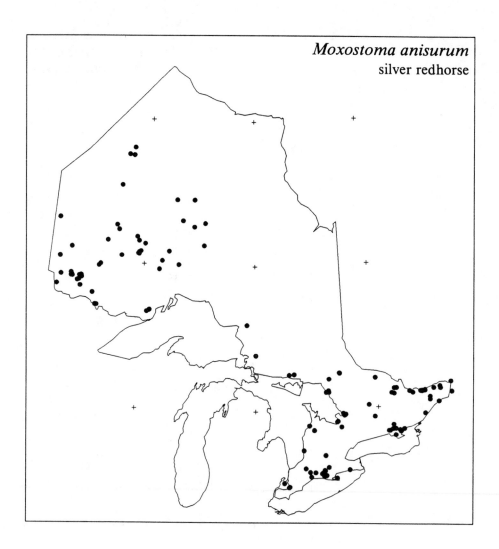

Moxostoma anisurum
silver redhorse

Moxostoma carinatum
river redhorse

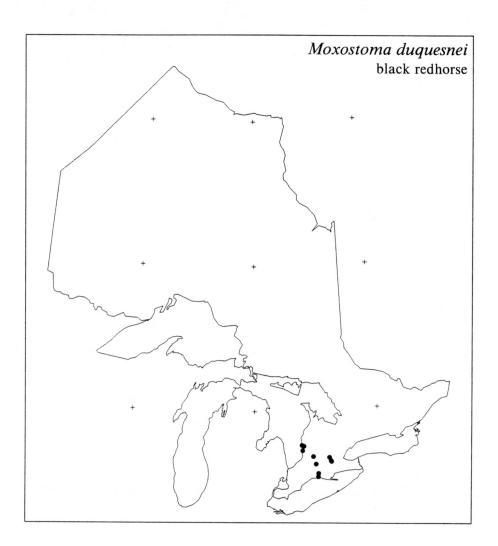

Moxostoma duquesnei
black redhorse

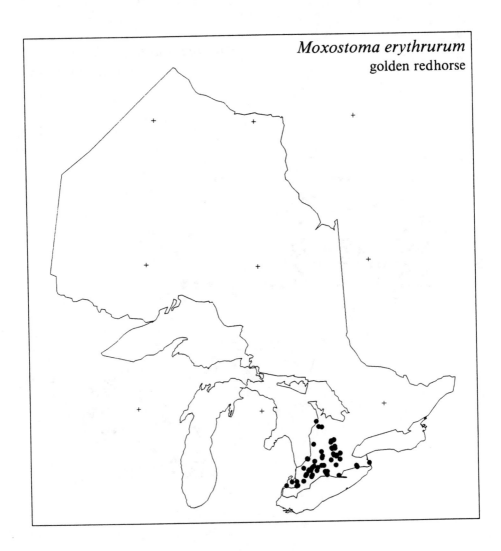

Moxostoma erythrurum
golden redhorse

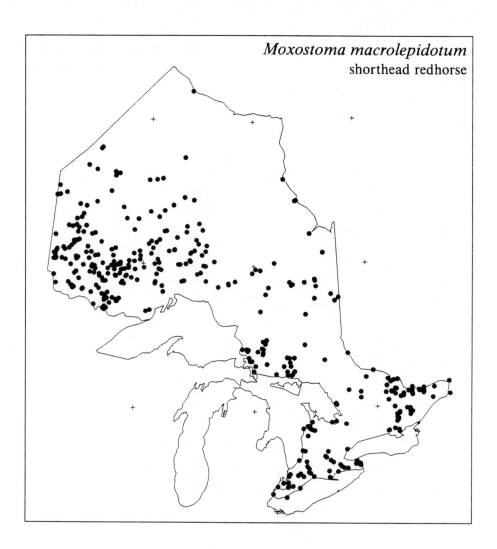

Moxostoma macrolepidotum
shorthead redhorse

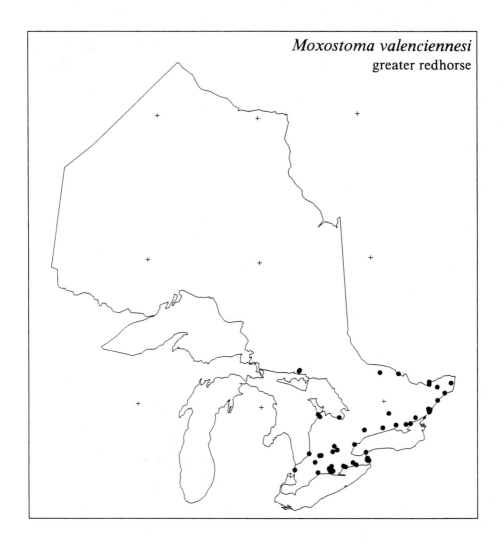

Moxostoma valenciennesi
greater redhorse

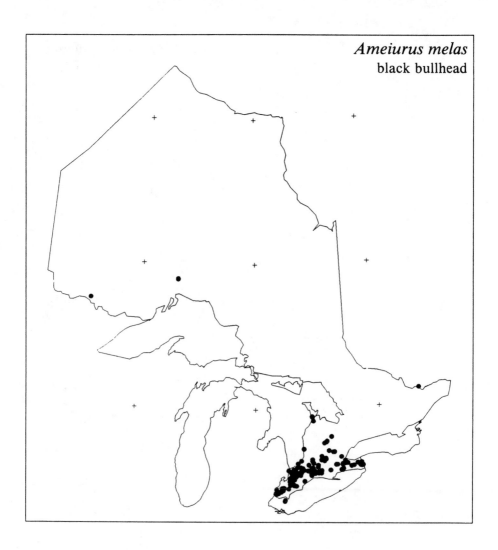

Ameiurus melas
black bullhead

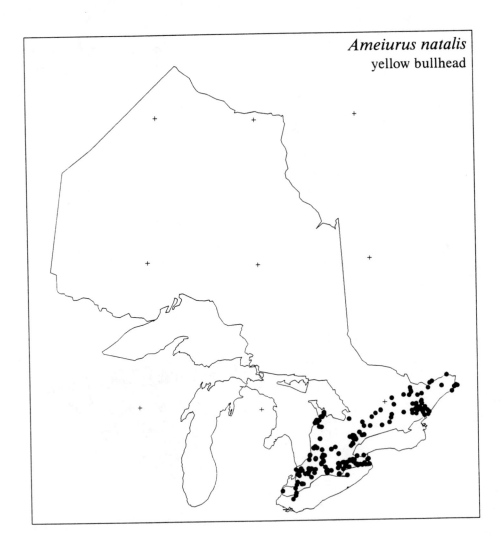

Ameiurus natalis
yellow bullhead

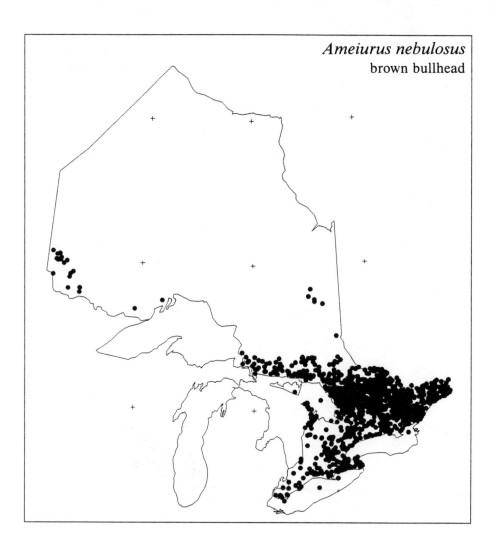

Ameiurus nebulosus
brown bullhead

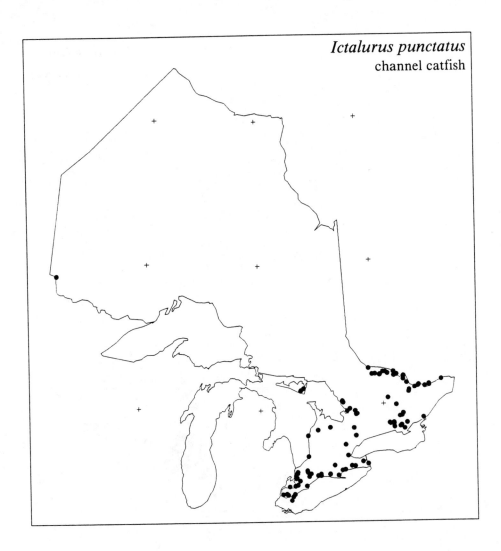

Ictalurus punctatus
channel catfish

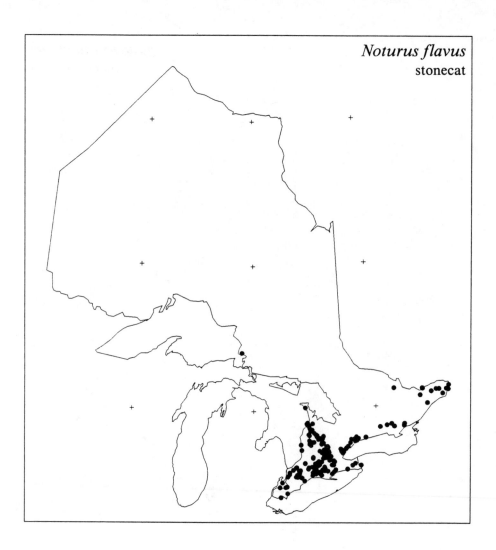

Noturus flavus
stonecat

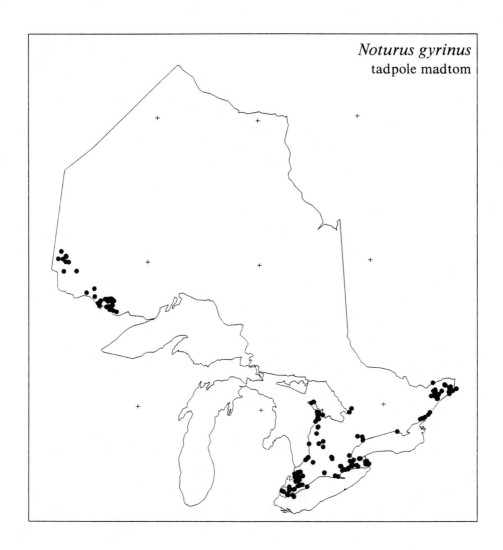

Noturus gyrinus
tadpole madtom

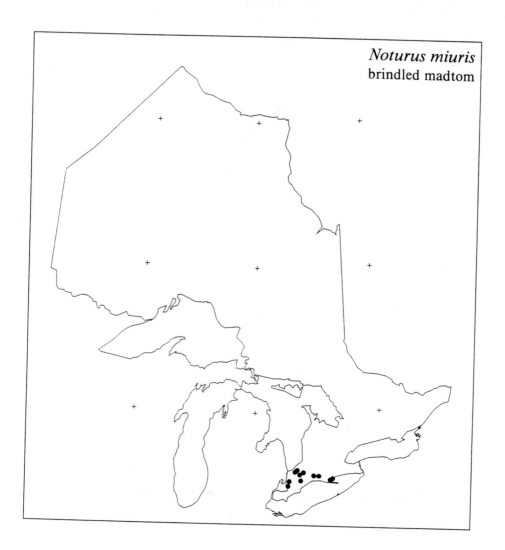

Noturus miuris
brindled madtom

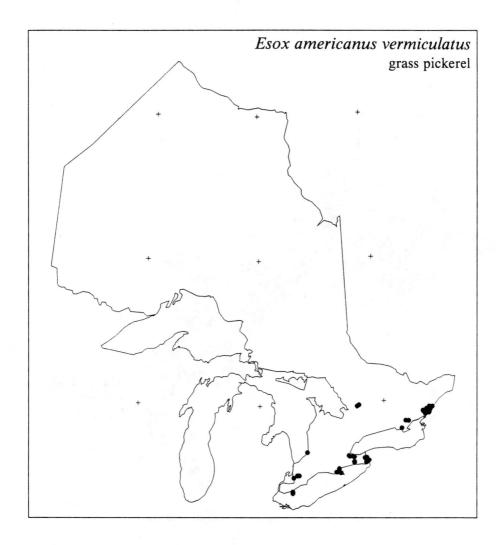

Esox americanus vermiculatus
grass pickerel

93

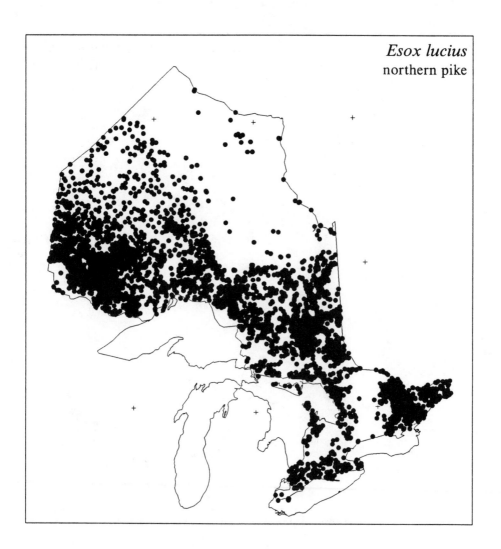

Esox lucius
northern pike

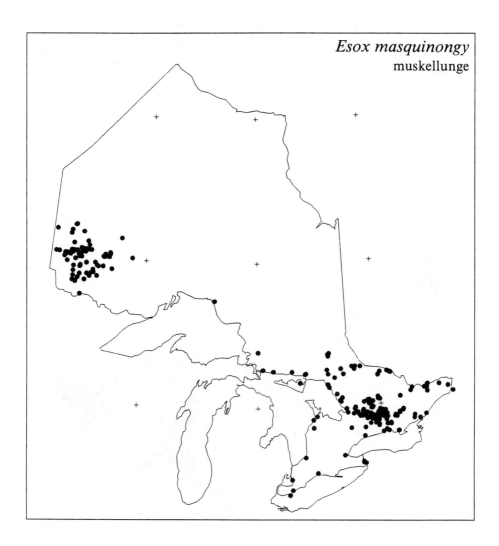

Esox masquinongy
muskellunge

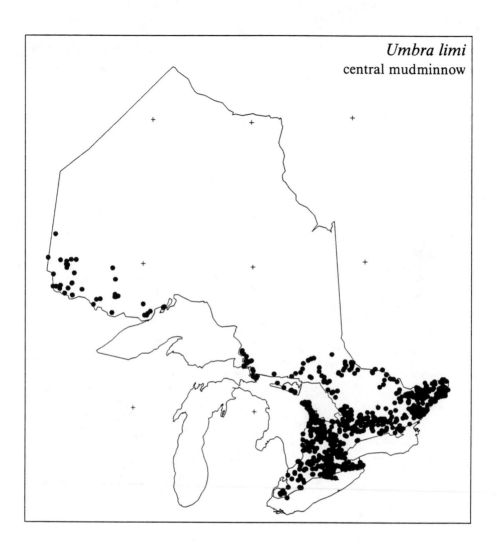

Umbra limi
central mudminnow

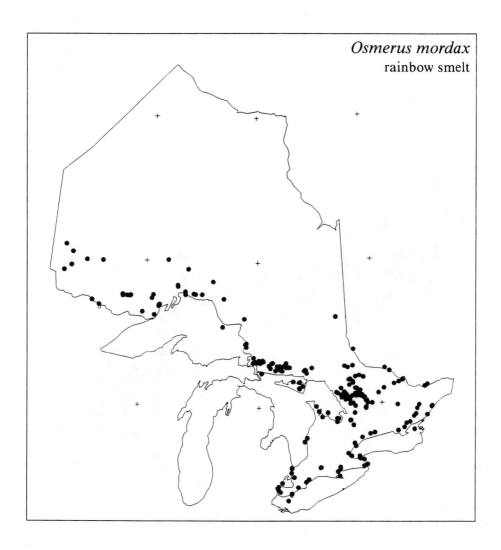

Osmerus mordax
rainbow smelt

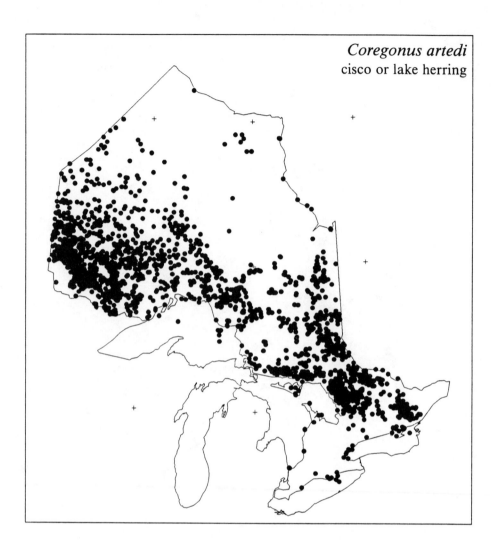

Coregonus artedi
cisco or lake herring

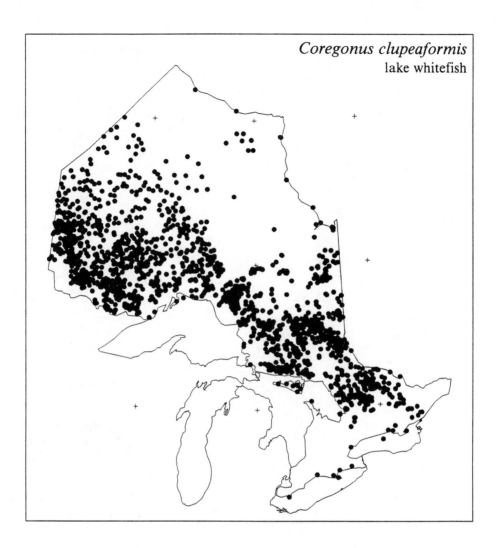

Coregonus clupeaformis
lake whitefish

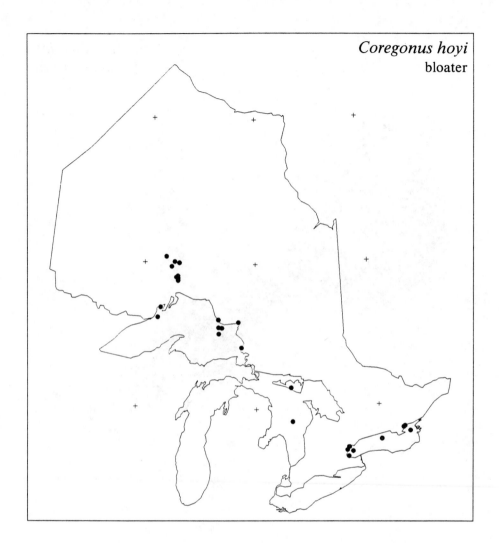

Coregonus hoyi
bloater

Coregonus johannae
deepwater cisco

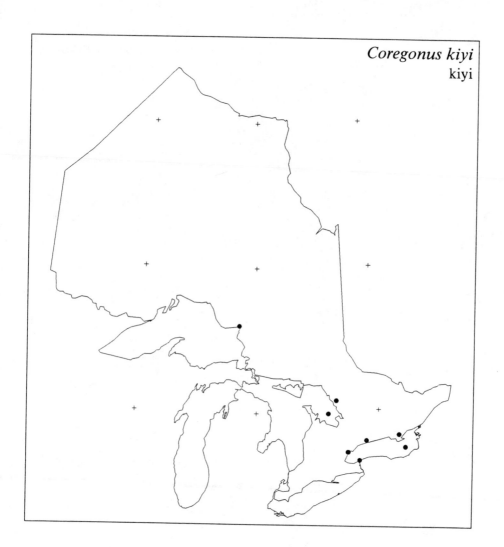

Coregonus kiyi
kiyi

Coregonus nigripinnis
blackfin cisco

Coregonus reighardi
shortnose cisco

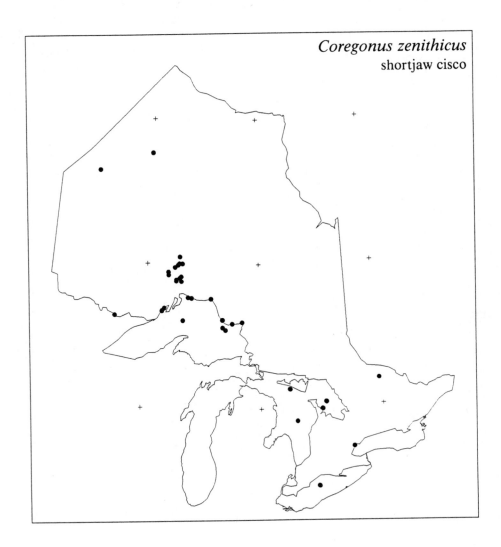

Coregonus zenithicus
shortjaw cisco

Oncorhynchus gorbuscha
pink salmon

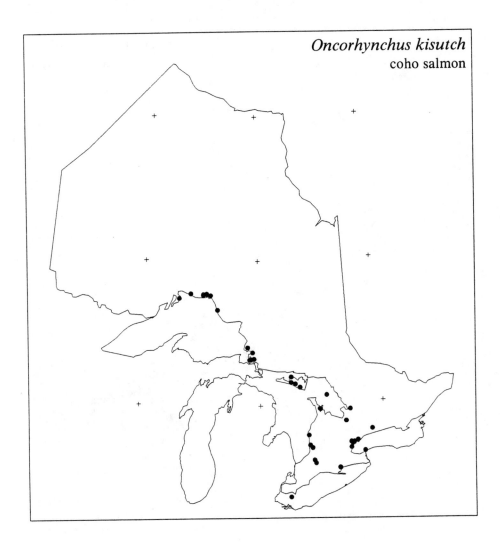

Oncorhynchus kisutch
coho salmon

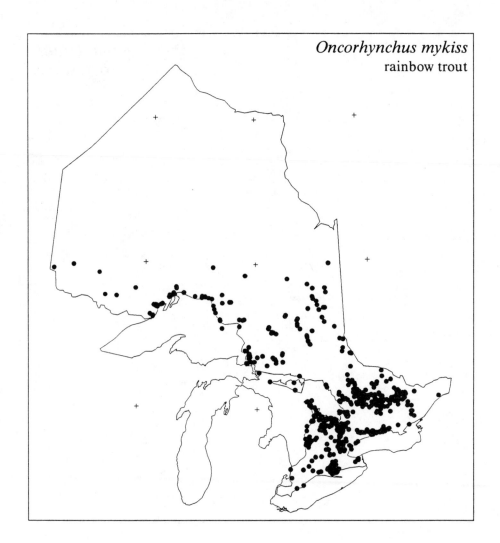

Oncorhynchus mykiss
rainbow trout

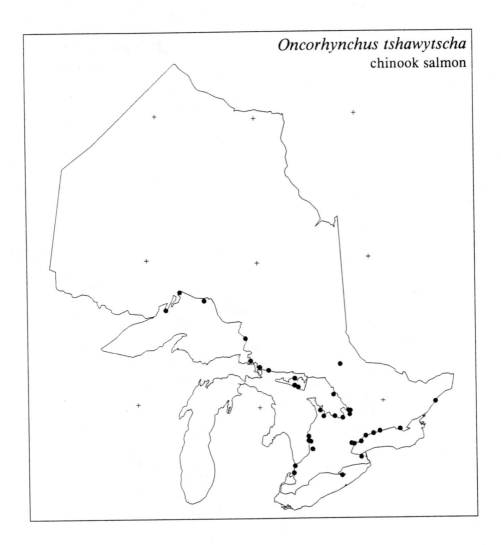

Oncorhynchus tshawytscha
chinook salmon

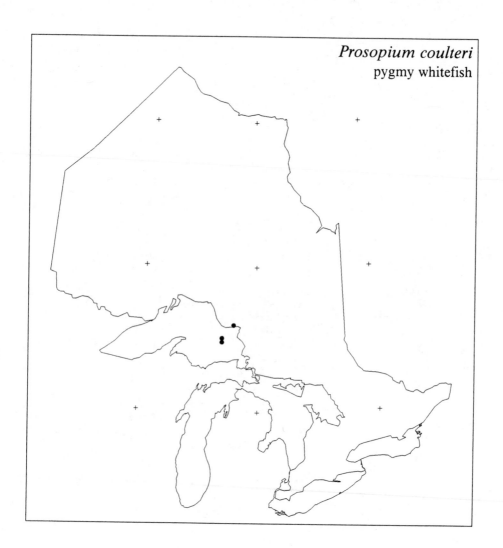

Prosopium coulteri
pygmy whitefish

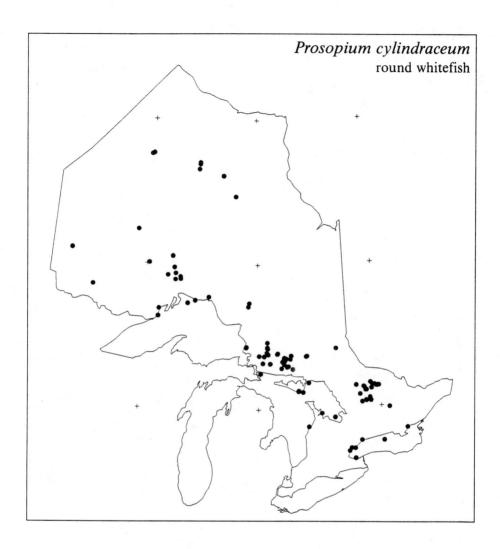

Prosopium cylindraceum
round whitefish

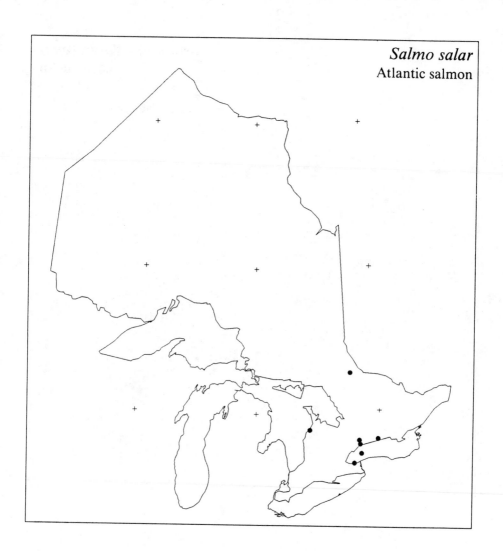

Salmo salar
Atlantic salmon

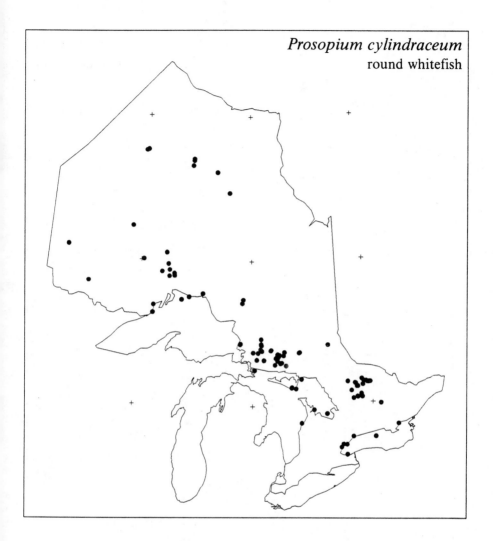

Prosopium cylindraceum
round whitefish

Salmo salar
Atlantic salmon

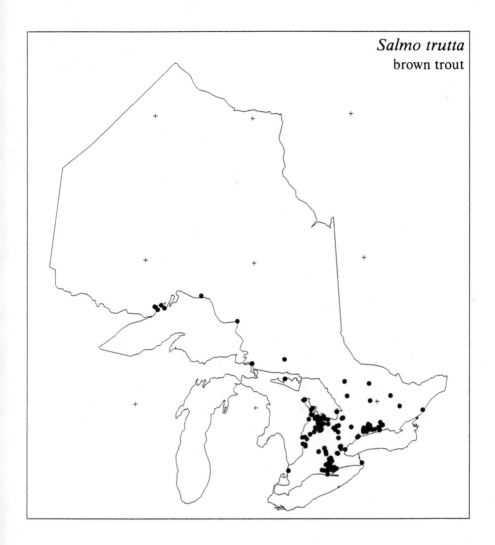

Salmo trutta
brown trout

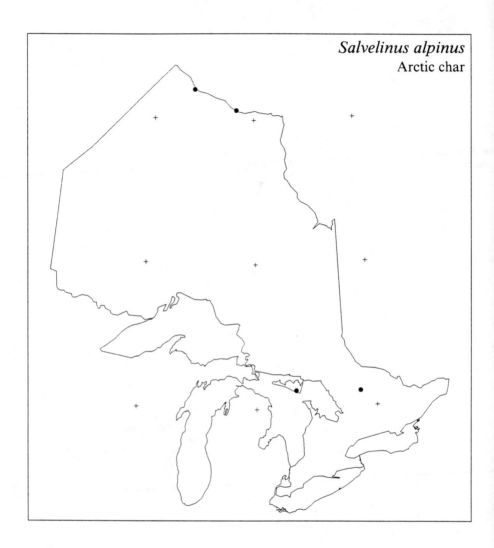

Salvelinus alpinus
Arctic char

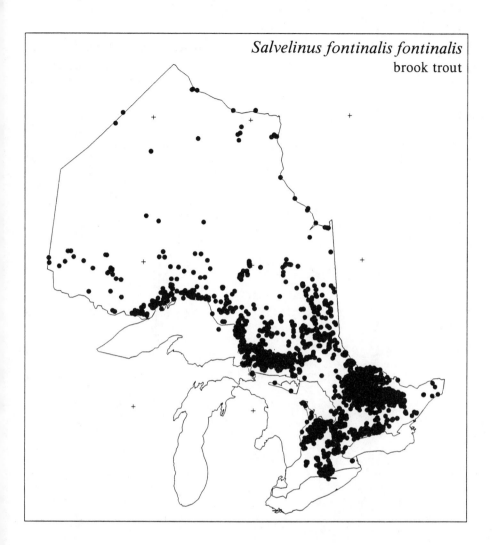

Salvelinus fontinalis fontinalis
brook trout

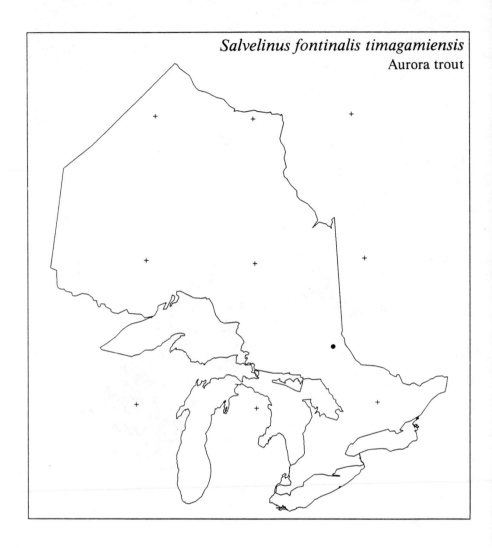

Salvelinus fontinalis timagamiensis
Aurora trout

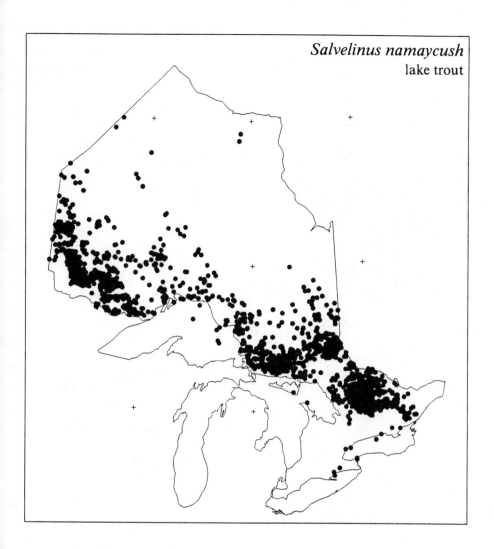

Salvelinus namaycush
lake trout

117

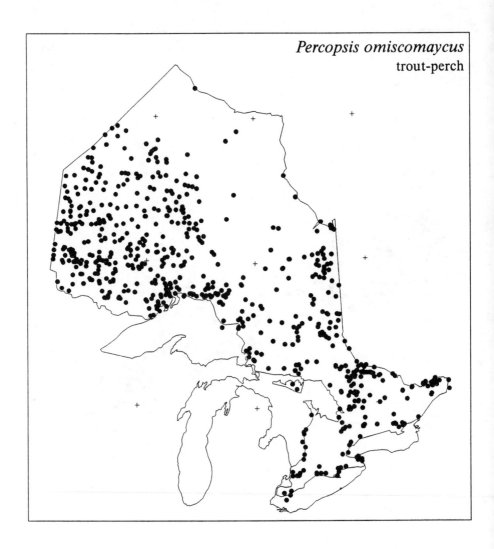

Percopsis omiscomaycus
trout-perch

118

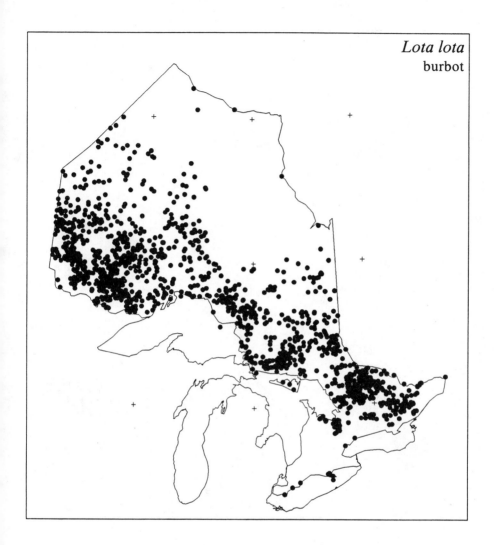

Lota lota
burbot

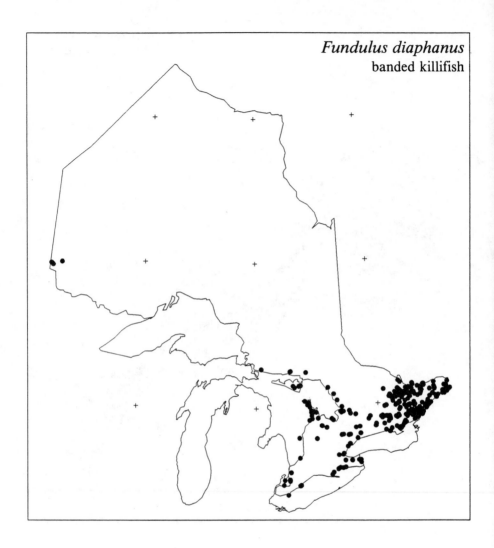

Fundulus diaphanus
banded killifish

120

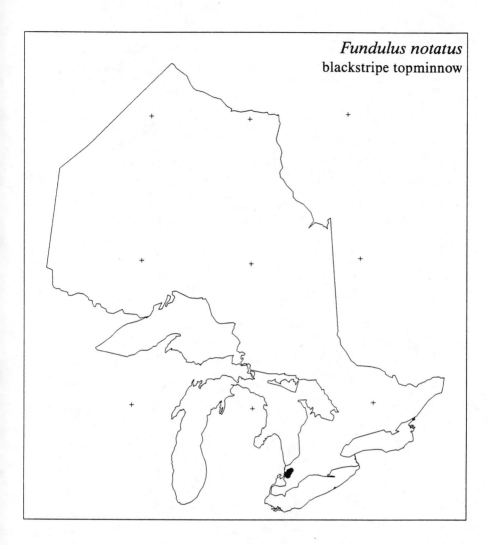

Fundulus notatus
blackstripe topminnow

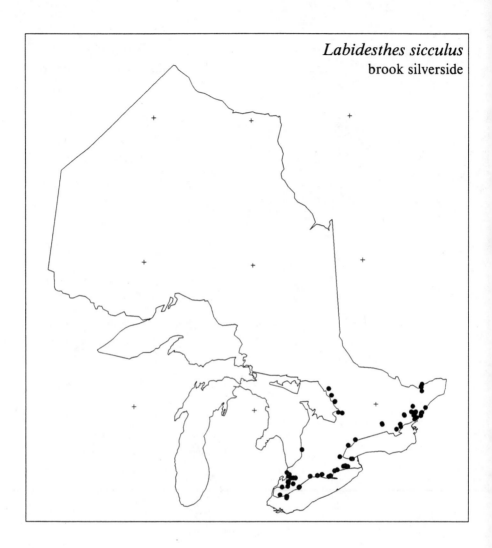

Labidesthes sicculus
brook silverside

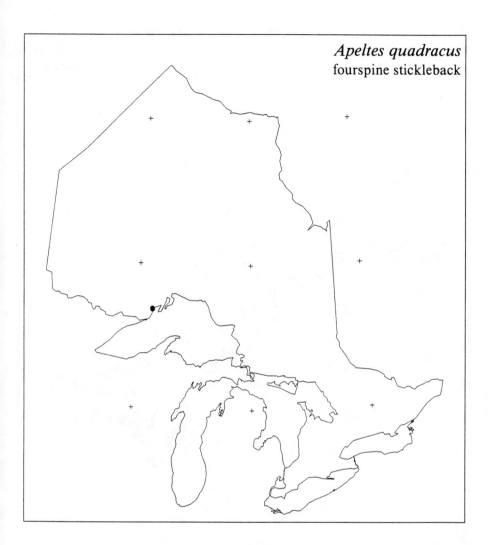

Apeltes quadracus
fourspine stickleback

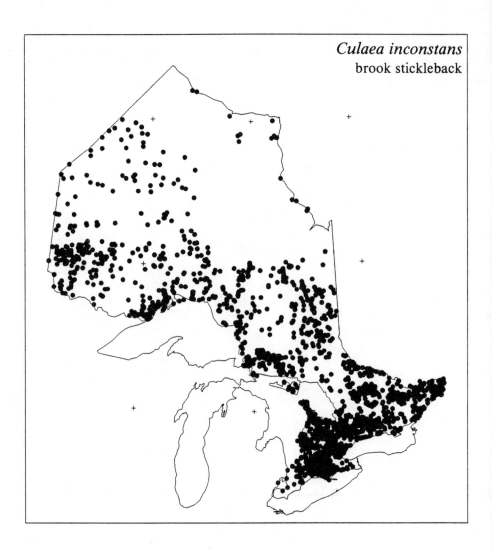

Culaea inconstans
brook stickleback

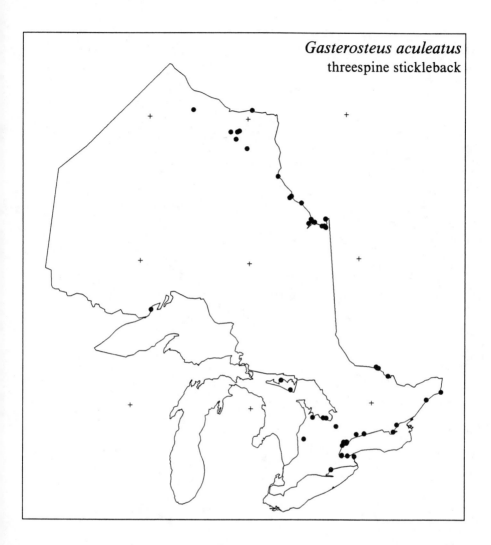

Gasterosteus aculeatus
threespine stickleback

125

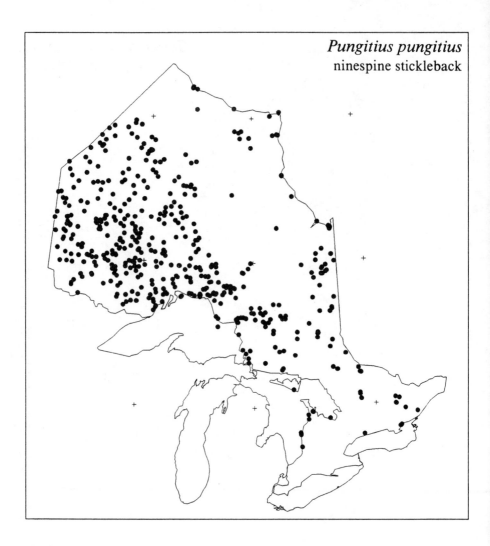

Pungitius pungitius
ninespine stickleback

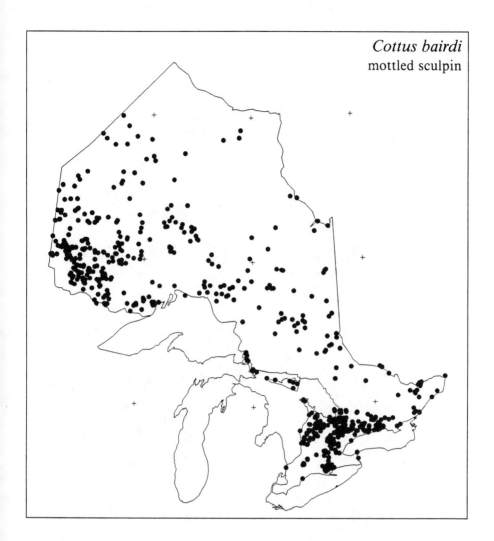

Cottus bairdi
mottled sculpin

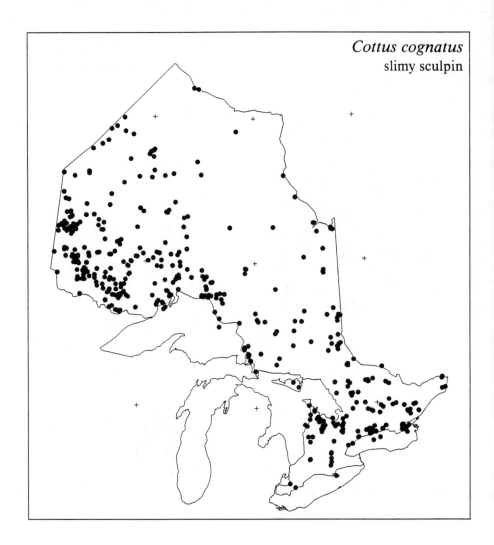

Cottus cognatus
slimy sculpin

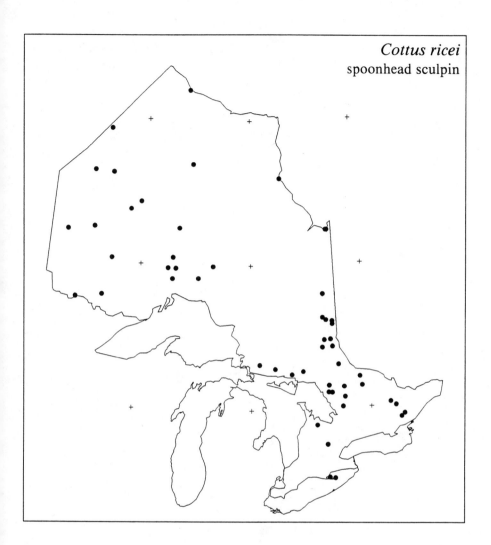

Cottus ricei
spoonhead sculpin

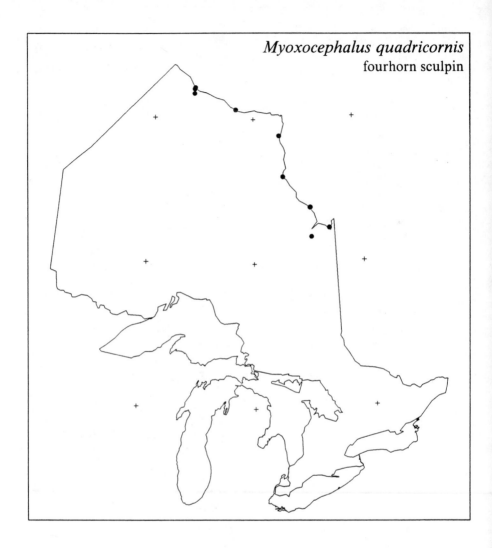

Myoxocephalus quadricornis
fourhorn sculpin

Myoxocephalus thompsoni
deepwater sculpin

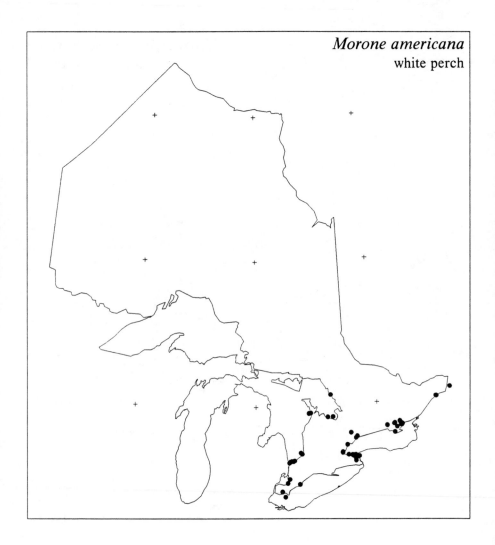

Morone americana
white perch

Morone chrysops
white bass

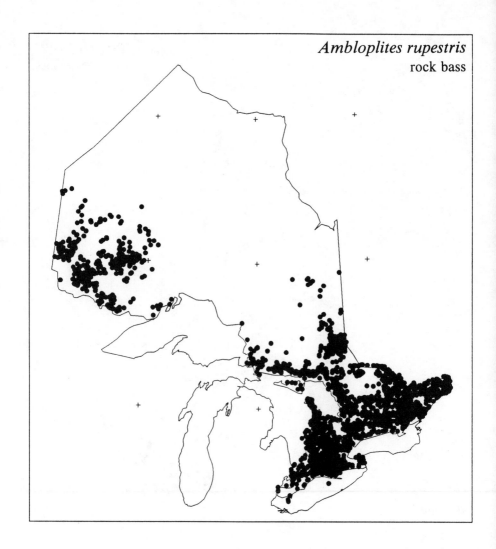

Ambloplites rupestris
rock bass

134

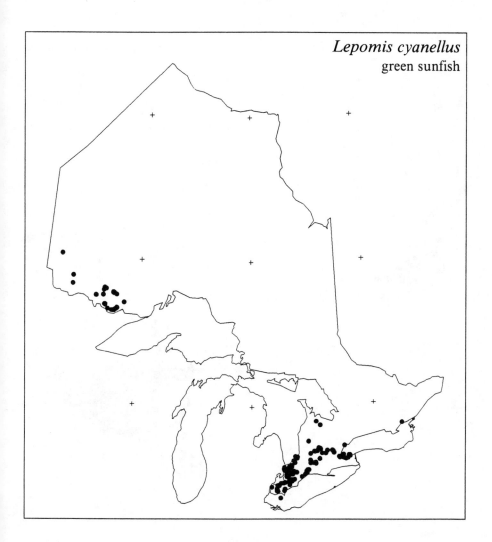

Lepomis cyanellus
green sunfish

135

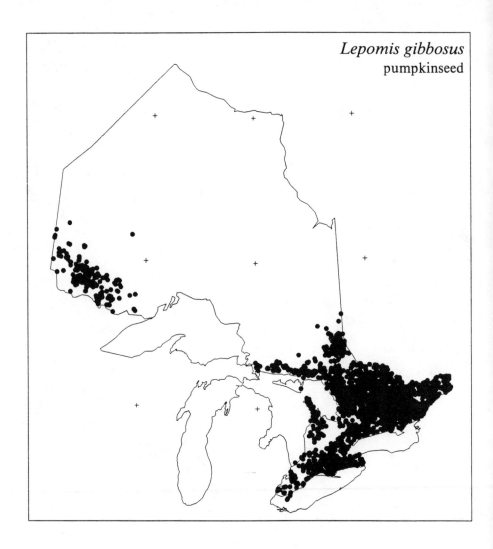

Lepomis gibbosus
pumpkinseed

Lepomis gulosus
warmouth

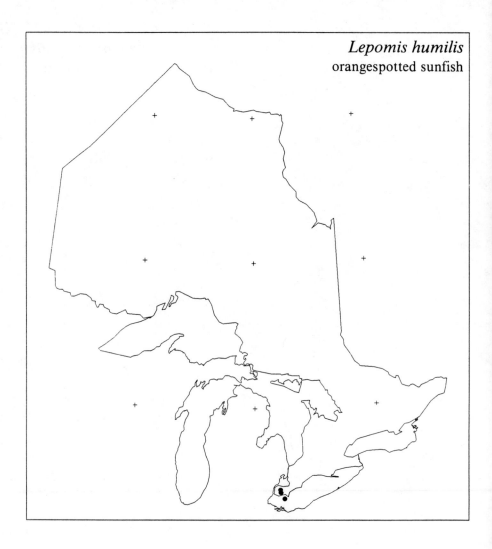

Lepomis humilis
orangespotted sunfish

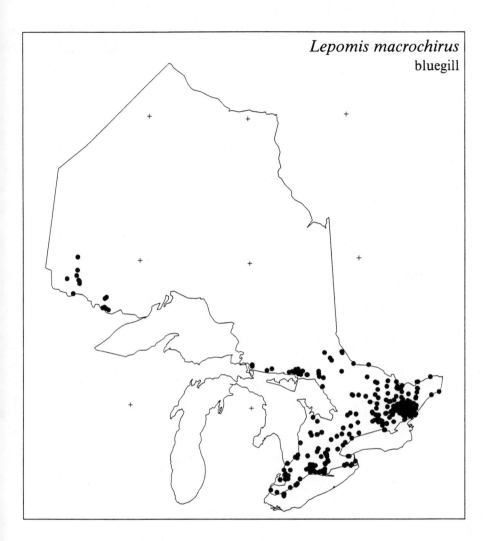

Lepomis macrochirus
bluegill

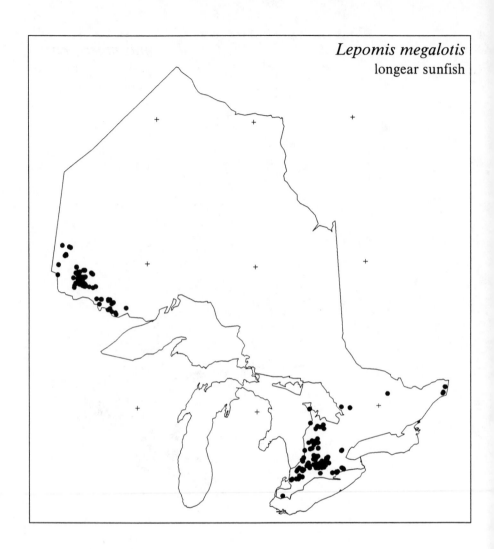

Lepomis megalotis
longear sunfish

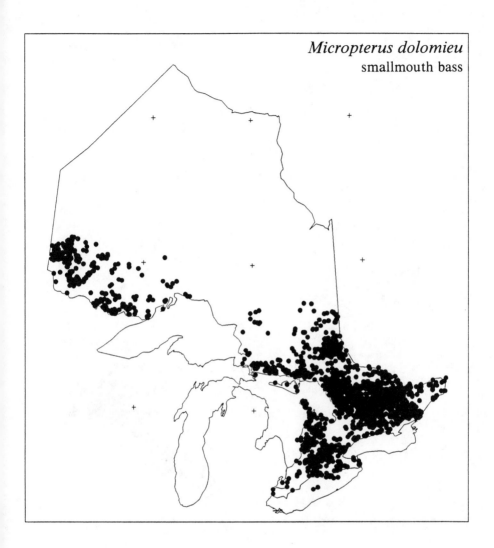

Micropterus dolomieu
smallmouth bass

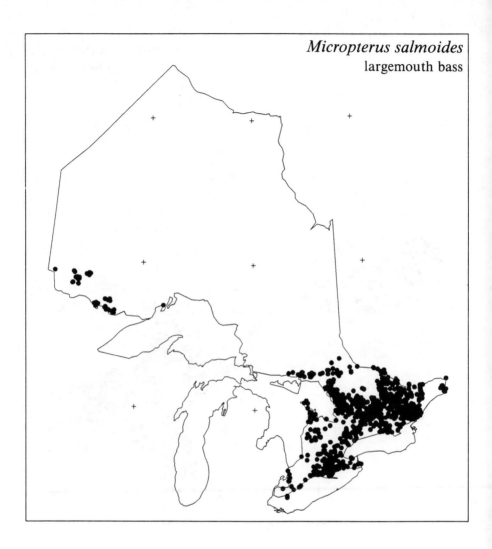

Micropterus salmoides
largemouth bass

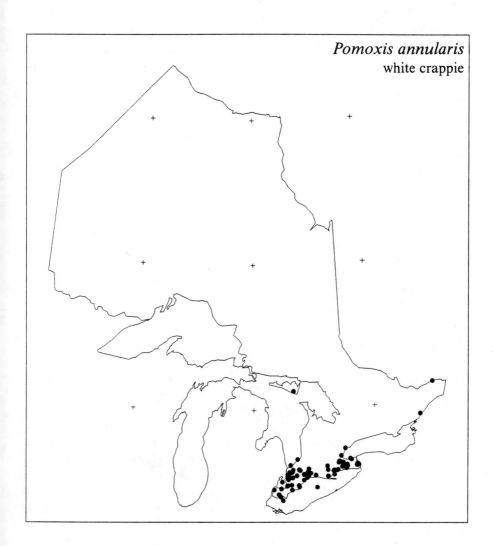

Pomoxis annularis
white crappie

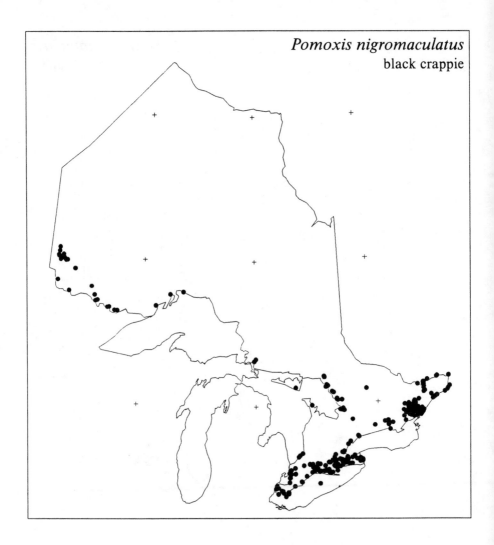

Pomoxis nigromaculatus
black crappie

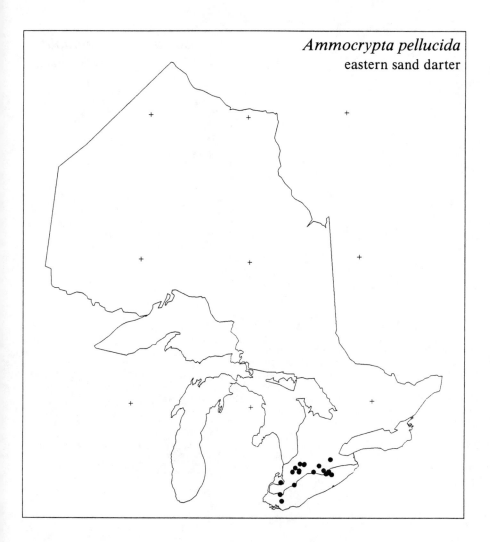

Ammocrypta pellucida
eastern sand darter

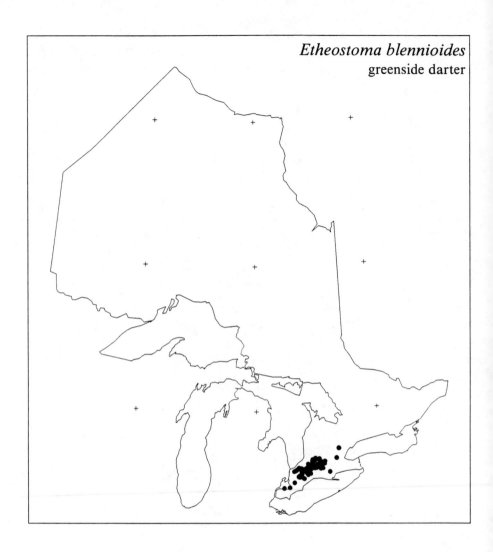

Etheostoma blennioides
greenside darter

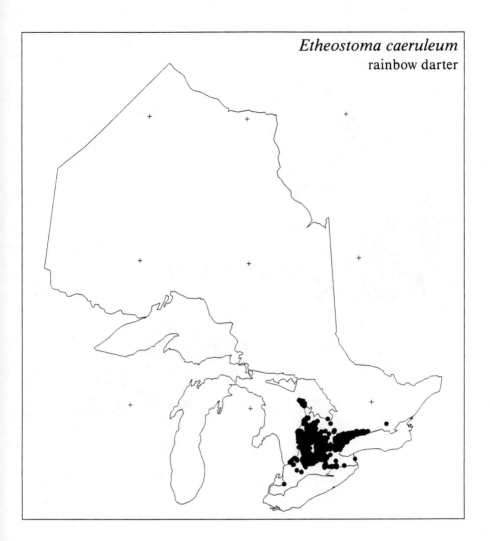

Etheostoma caeruleum
rainbow darter

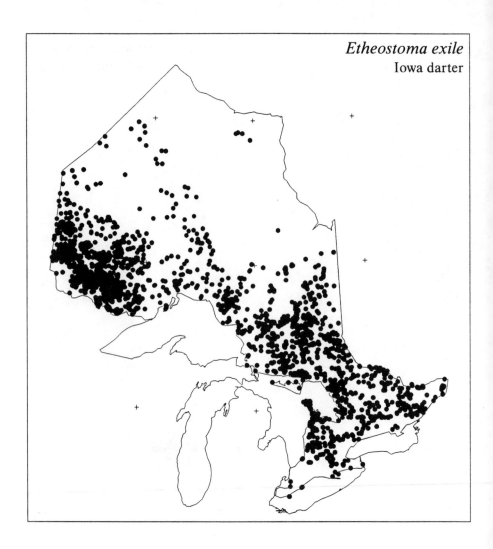

Etheostoma exile
Iowa darter

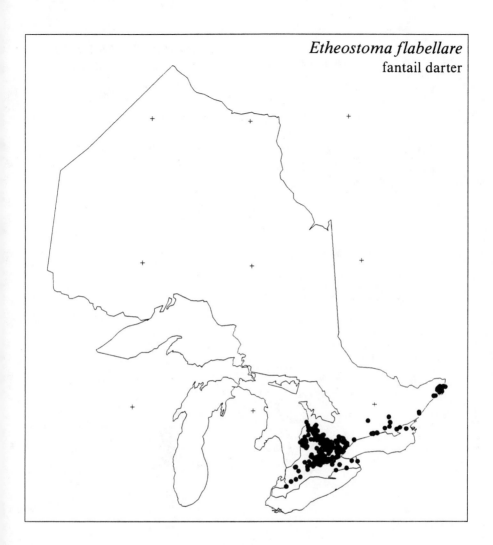

Etheostoma flabellare
fantail darter

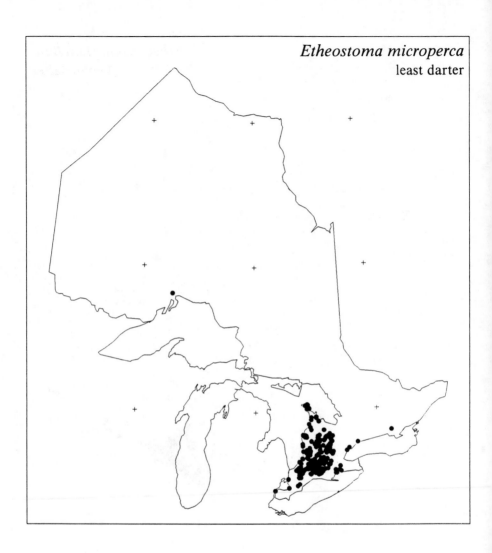

Etheostoma microperca
least darter

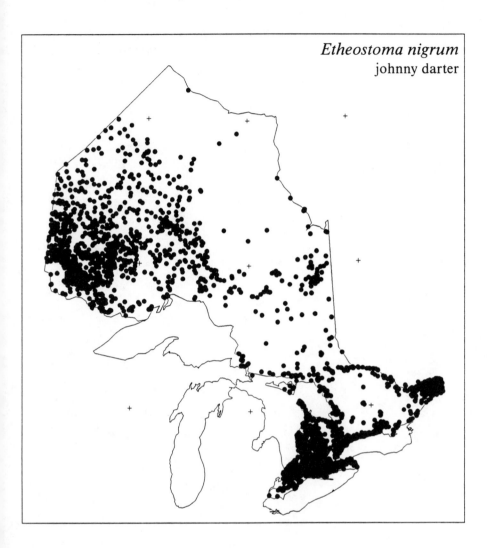

Etheostoma nigrum
johnny darter

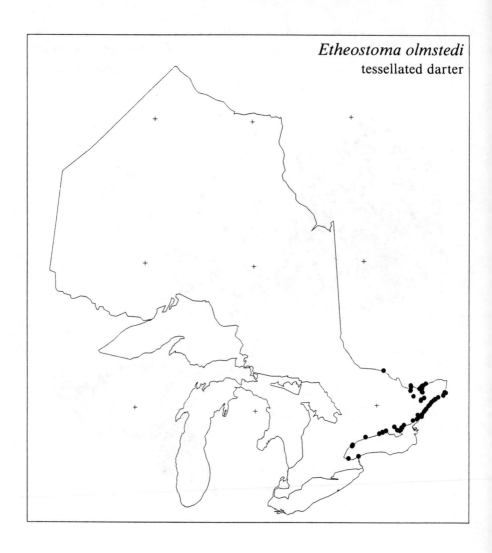

Etheostoma olmstedi
tessellated darter

152

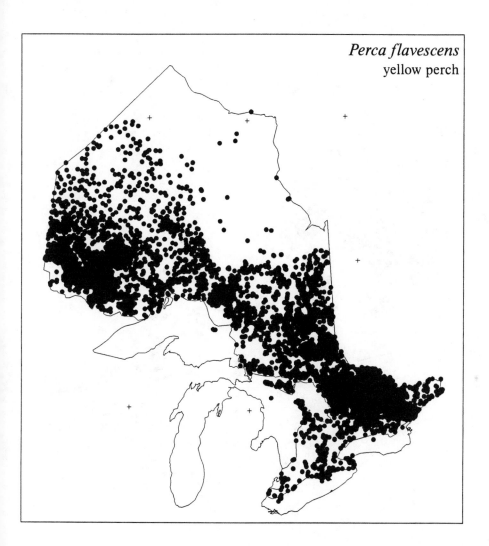

Perca flavescens
yellow perch

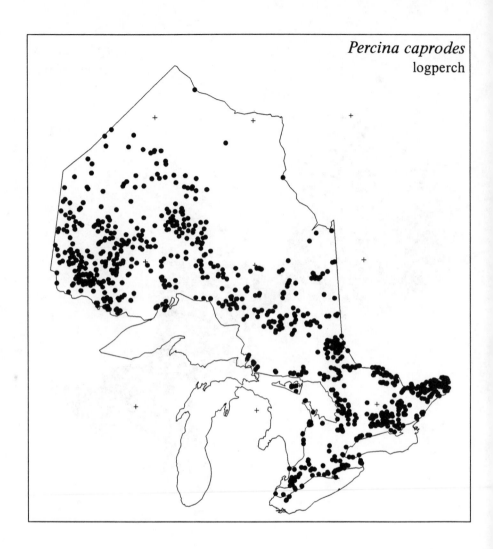

Percina caprodes
logperch

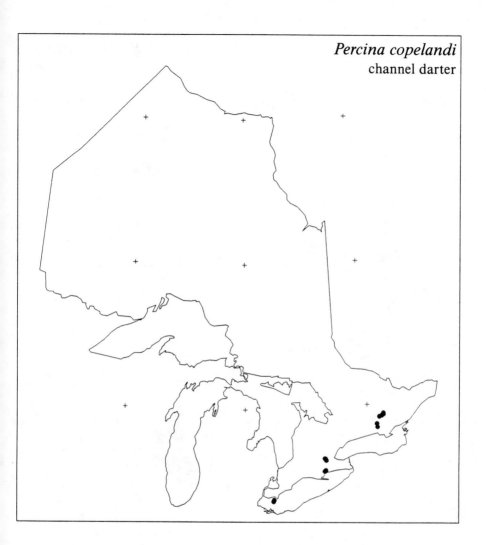

Percina copelandi
channel darter

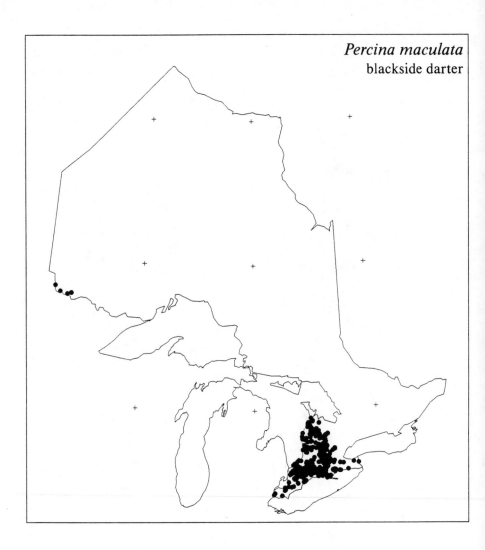

Percina maculata
blackside darter

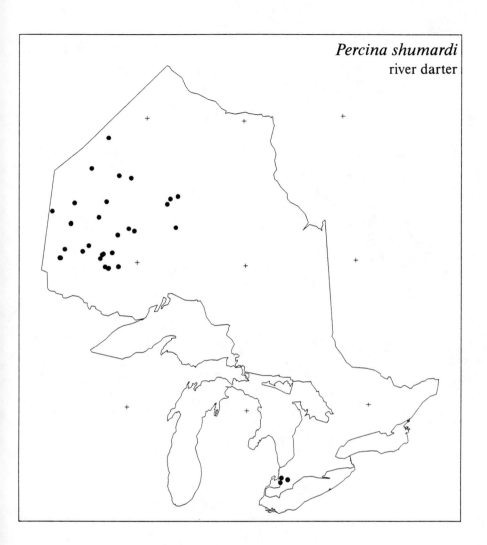

Percina shumardi
river darter

157

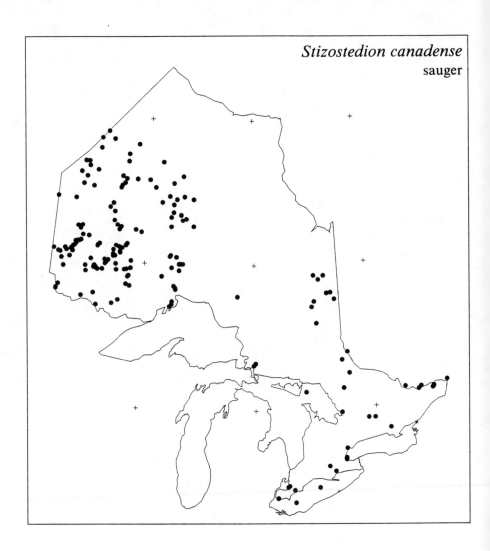

Stizostedion canadense
sauger

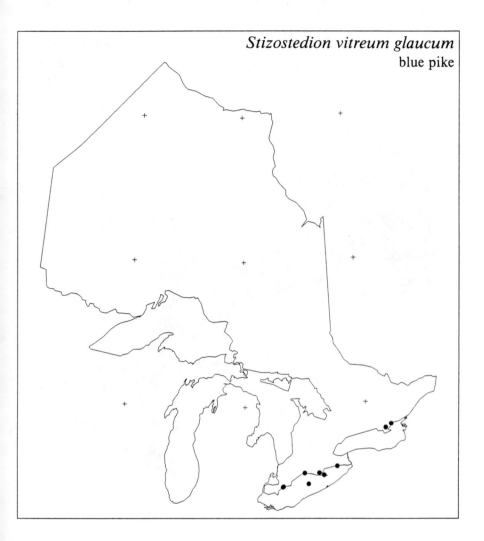

Stizostedion vitreum glaucum
blue pike

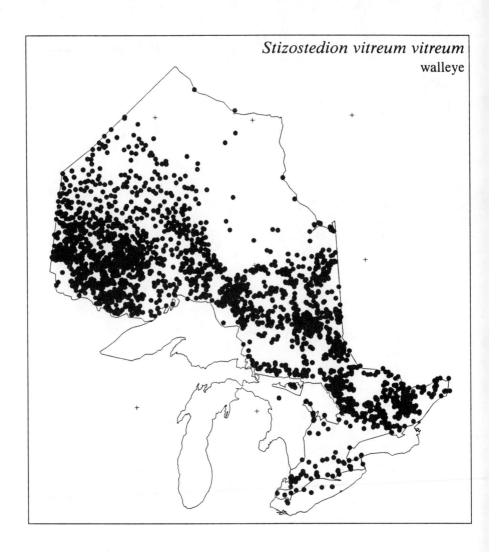

Stizostedion vitreum vitreum
walleye

Aplodinotus grunniens
freshwater drum

ACKNOWLEDGEMENTS

We would like to thank Mr. E. Holm of the Department of Ichthyology and Herpetology, Royal Ontario Museum (ROM), and the other members of the department for their assistance in many aspects of this study. Mr. G. Gale of Fisheries Branch, Ontario Ministry of Natural Resources (OMNR), lent both his time and resources. Mr. W. Felhmer of University of Toronto Computing Services provided computer programming support. Additional distribution data were provided by the Canadian Museum of Nature, University of Michigan Museum of Zoology, and various OMNR District Offices.

Our thanks go as well to the ROM Publications and Print Services Department for their work on the book, particularly to Kat Mototsune for the editing.

Financial support was provided to E. J. Crossman by Fisheries Branch, OMNR, to computerize the Ontario fish records of the ROM and transfer them to the OMNR FSDDS. Financial support was also provided by an OMNR Ontario Renewable Resources Research Grant Programme grant to E. J. Crossman, and by University of Toronto Open Fellowships to N. E. Mandrak.

APPENDICES

Appendix 1

Changes in the Scientific Names of Ontario Freshwater Fishes since 1980

There are several changes in scientific names of Ontario freshwater fishes since Robins et al. (1980). These result from recent studies that have developed new concepts of relationships between groups of species, or that have revealed the existence of older valid names. Most of these changes are in the family Cyprinidae, the carps and minnows. The list below provides the names used in Robins et al. (1980), and the equivalent names found in Robins et al. (1991) which are used in this checklist.

Robins et al., 1980	Robins et al., 1991
Coregonus alpenae	*Coregonus zenithicus*
Salmo gairdneri	*Oncorhynchus mykiss*
Hybopsis storeriana	*Macrhybopsis storeriana*
Hybopsis x-punctata	*Erimystax x-punctatus*
Notropis chrysocephalus	*Luxilus chrysocephalus*
Notropis cornutus	*Luxilus cornutus*
Notropis emiliae	*Opsopoeodus emiliae*
Notropis spilopterus	*Cyprinella spiloptera*
Notropis umbratilis	*Lythrurus umbratilis*
Semotilus margarita	*Margariscus margarita*
Ictalurus melas	*Ameiurus melas*
Ictalurus natalis	*Ameiurus natalis*
Ictalurus nebulosus	*Ameiurus nebulosus*

Appendix 2

Instructions on Preparing and Forwarding Information on the Ontario Fish Fauna

As the study of the composition and distribution of Ontario fishes is ongoing at the Royal Ontario Museum, we welcome and encourage the submission of any relevant new information not contained in this publication. This would include information on species collected in Ontario but not included in the checklist, and listed species collected from locations not recorded on the maps. In order for this information to be most useful the precise location and date of capture, and a specimen used to verify the species identity, are required. This voucher specimen would be deposited in the ROM ichthyology collection. The best ways for preparing specimens for shipment are as follows (after Scott and Crossman, 1973a):

1. Alcohol Preservation—liquids with high alcoholic content, such as rubbing alcohol, can be used. Fish should be immersed in the liquid as quickly as possible after capture. Specimens over 15 cm in length should be slit (two three-centimetre slits, in lower right side) in order to allow the preservative to enter the body cavity. The fish should be left in the liquid for 7–10 days depending on size. It can then be removed, wrapped in a wet cloth, placed in a waterproof plastic bag, and packaged adequately for shipment.

2. Freezing—specimens can be wrapped in a plastic bag and hard frozen in a freezer. The fish should be packed in ice (preferably dry ice) and placed in an insulated container for shipping.

3. Salting—fish can be preserved by packing the body cavity with salt. Specimens should then be placed in a waterproof plastic bag and forwarded immediately. As an alternative, fish can be immersed for several days in a strong brine solution (at least 100 grams of salt per litre of water). Body cavity must be opened to allow rapid entry of salt solution. Shipping instructions are the same as for alcohol-preserved specimens.

Specimens should be sent with accompanying documentation. Alcohol-preserved and salted specimens can be sent by first-class mail. Frozen specimens must be sent by courier or delivered in person to Department of Ichthyology and Herpetology, Royal Ontario Museum, 100 Queen's Park, Toronto, Ontario, M5S 2C6, (416) 586-5759.

N.B. Specimens should be forwarded only after prior arrangement with the recipient.

LITERATURE CITED

AGASSIZ, L.
1850   Lake Superior: its physical character, vegetation and animals. Boston, Gould, Kendall and Lincoln. 428 pp. (Reprint. New York, Arno Press, 1970).

BENSLEY, B. A.
1915   The fishes of Georgian Bay. *In* Contributions to Canadian Biology, being studies from the biological stations of Canada 1911–1914, fasc. 2 - Freshwater fish and lake biology, pp. 1–51. Supplement to the 47th annual report of the Dept. of Marine Fisheries, Fisheries Branch. Ottawa, King's Printer.

BERST, A. H. and G. R. SPANGLER
1973   Lake Huron - The ecology of the fish community and man's effects on it. Great Lakes Fishery Commission Technical Report 21. 41 pp.

BOWLBY, J. N. and D. GREEN
1987   Efficiency of aquatic habitat inventory surveys in the assessment of fish species present. Ontario Ministry of Natural Resources, Fisheries Acidification Technical Report 87-08. 39 pp.

CAMPBELL, R. R.
1991   Rare and endangered fishes and marine mammals of Canada: COSEWIC Fish and Marine Mammal Subcommittee status reports: VII. Canadian Field-Naturalist 105:151–156.

CHRISTIE, W. J.
1973   A review of the changes in the fish species composition of Lake Ontario. Great Lakes Fishery Commission Technical Report 23. 65 pp.

COAD, B. W.
1987   Checklist of the fishes of the Ottawa District. Trail and Landscape 21(1):40–59.

COX, E. T.
1978   Counts and measurements of Ontario lakes. Toronto, Ontario Ministry of Natural Resources, Fisheries Branch. 114 pp.

CROSSMAN, E. J.
1976   Quetico fishes. Life Sciences Miscellaneous Publications. Toronto, Royal Ontario Museum. 86 pp.

CROSSMAN, E. J. and E. HOLM
1978   A revised list of Ontario freshwater fishes. Information leaflet. Toronto, Royal Ontario Museum, Dept. of Ichthyology and Herpetology. 8 pp.

CROSSMAN, E. J. and H. D. Van METER
1979   Annotated list of the fishes of the Lake Ontario watershed. Great Lakes Fishery Commission Technical Report 36. 25 pp.

CURRAN, H. W., J. BARDACH, R. I. BOWMAN, and H. G. LAWLER
1947   A biological survey of Lake Opinicon. Progress Report of the Queen's University Biological Station. Kingston, Hanson and Edgar. 48 pp.

165

DODGE, D. P., G. A. GOODCHILD, J. C. TILT, and D. C. WALDRIFF
  1984   Manual of instructions - aquatic habitat inventory surveys. 6th ed. rev.
          Toronto, Ontario Ministry of Natural Resources, Fisheries Branch. 168 pp.
DYMOND, J. R.
  1922   A provisional list of the fishes of Lake Erie. Publications of the Ontario
          Fisheries Research Laboratory 4:57–73.
  1926   The fishes of Lake Nipigon. Publications of the Ontario Fisheries Research
          Laboratory 27. 108 pp.
  1939   The fishes of the Ottawa region. Contributions of the Royal Ontario
          Museum of Zoology 15. 43 pp.
  1947   A list of the freshwater fishes of Canada east of the Rocky Mountains.
          Royal Ontario Museum of Zoology, Miscellaneous Publications 1. 36 pp.
DYMOND, J. R. and J. L. HART
  1927   The fishes of Lake Abitibi (Ontario) and adjacent waters. Publications of
          the Ontario Fisheries Research Laboratory 28. 19 pp.
DYMOND, J. R. and W. B. SCOTT
  1941   Fishes of Patricia Portion of the Kenora District, Ontario. Copeia
          1941(4):243–245.
DYMOND, J. R., J. L. HART, and A. L. PRITCHARD
  1929   The fishes of the Canadian waters of Lake Ontario. Publications of the
          Ontario Fisheries Research Laboratory 37. 35 pp.

EVERMANN, B. W. and E. L. GOLDSBOROUGH
  1907   A checklist of the freshwater fishes of Canada. Proceedings of the
          Biological Society of Washington 22:185–188.
EVERMANN, B. W. and H. B. LATIMER
  1910   The fishes of the Lake of the Woods and connecting waters. Proceedings of
          the United States National Museum 39:121–136.

HALKETT, A.
  1913   Checklist of the fishes of the Dominion of Canada and Newfoundland.
          Ottawa, King's Printer. 138 pp.
HARTMAN, W. L.
  1973   Effects of exploitation, environmental changes, and new species on the fish
          habitats and resources of Lake Erie. Great Lakes Fishery Commission
          Technical Report 22. 43 pp.
HARTVIKSEN, C. and W. MOMOT
  1989   Fishes of the Thunder Bay area of Ontario. Thunder Bay, Wildwood
          Publications. 282 pp.
HUBBS, C. L. and D. E. S. BROWN
  1929   Materials for a distributional study of Ontario fishes. Transactions of the
          Royal Canadian Institute 17:1–56.
HUBBS, C. L. and K. F. LAGLER
  1964   Fishes of the Great Lakes Region. Reprint. Bulletin 26. Toronto,
          Ambassador Books. 213 pp.

LAWRIE, A. H. and J. F. RAHRER
  1973   Lake Superior - A case history of the lake and its fisheries. Great Lakes
          Fishery Commission Technical Report 19. 69 pp.

166

LEE, D. S., C. R. GILBERT, C. H. HOCUTT, R. E. JENKINS, D. E. McALLISTER, and
J. R. STAUFFER, Jr.
  1980   Atlas of North American freshwater fishes. North Carolina Biological
          Survey Publication 1980-12. North Carolina State Museum of Natural
          History. 867 pp.
LINDEBORG, R. G.
  1941   Records of fishes from the Quetico Provincial Park of Ontario, with
          comments on the growth of the yellow pike-perch. Copeia 1941(3):159–161.

MacCRIMMON, H. R. and E. SKOBE
  1970   The fisheries of Lake Simcoe. Toronto, Ontario Dept. of Lands and
          Forests, Fish and Wildlife Branch. 140 pp.
MACINS, V.
  1972   The fisheries of Lake of the Woods. Toronto, Ontario, Ministry of Natural
          Resources, Sport Fisheries Branch. 44 pp.
MANDRAK, N. E.
  1990   The zoogeography of Ontario freshwater fishes. Unpublished MSc. thesis,
          University of Toronto. 190 pp.
MARTIN, N. V. and F. E. J. FRY
  1973   Lake Opeongo - The ecology of the fish community and man's effects on it.
          Great Lakes Fishery Commission Technical Report 24. 34 pp.
McALLISTER, D. E. and B. W. COAD
  1974   Fishes of Canada's National Capital region. Canada Dept. of the
          Environment, Fisheries and Marine Service, Miscellaneous Special
          Publication 24. 200 pp.
MEEK, S. E. and H. W. CLARK
  1902   Notes on a collection of cold-blooded vertebrates from Ontario. Field
          Columbian Museum Publication 67, Zoological Series 3(7):131–149.
MEEK, S. E. and D. G. ELLIOT
  1899   Notes on the collection of fishes and amphibians from Muskoka and Gull
          Lakes. Field Columbian Museum Publication 41, Zoological Series
          1(17):307–311.
MILLER, P. J.
  1986   Gobiidae. In Whitehead, P. J. P., M. -L. Bauchot, J. -C. Jureau, J. Nielsen,
          and E. Tortonese, eds., Fishes of the North-eastern Atlantic and the
          Mediterranean. Paris, UNESCO, vol. 3, pp. 1019–1085.
MINNS, C. K.
  1986   A model of bias in lake selection for survey. Canadian Technical Report of
          Fisheries and Aquatic Sciences 1496. 21 pp.

NASH, C. W.
  1908   Manual of vertebrates of Ontario. Toronto, Warwick Brothers and Rutter.
          107 pp.
  1913   Fishes. In Faull, J. H., ed., The natural history of the Toronto region,
          Ontario, Canada. Toronto, Canadian Institute, pp. 249–271.

167

QADRI, S. U.
1968   Morphology and taxonomy of the aurora trout, *Salvelinus fontinalis timagamiensis*. National Museum of Canada Bulletin 237, Contributions to Zoology 5. 18 pp.

RADFORTH, I.
1944   Some considerations on the distribution of fishes in Ontario. Contributions of the Royal Ontario Museum of Zoology 25. 116 pp.

RICHARDSON, J.
1836   Fauna Boreali-Americana; or the zoology of the northern parts of British America: part third, the fish. London, Richard Bentley. 327 pp.

ROBINS, C. R., R. M. BAILEY, C. E. BOND, J. R. BROOKER, E. A. LACHNER, R. N. LEA, and W. B. SCOTT
1980   A list of common and scientific names of fishes from the United States and Canada. 4th ed. American Fisheries Society, Special Publication 12. 174 pp.
1991   A list of common and scientific names of fishes from the United States and Canada. 5th ed. American Fisheries Society, Special Publication 20. 183 pp.

RYDER, R. A., W. B. SCOTT, and E. J. CROSSMAN
1964   Fishes of northern Ontario, north of Albany River. Royal Ontario Museum, Life Sciences Contributions 60. 30 pp.

SAS INSTITUTE
1987   SAS/GRAPH Guide for Personal Computers, Version 6. Cary, SAS Institute Incorporated. 534 pp.

SCOTT, W. B.
1954   Freshwater fishes of eastern Canada. Toronto, University of Toronto Press. 137 pp.
1958   A checklist of the freshwater fishes of Canada and Alaska. Toronto, Royal Ontario Museum, Division of Zoology and Palaeontology. 30 pp.
1963   A review of the changes in the fish fauna of Ontario. Transactions of the Royal Canadian Institute 34:111–125.

SCOTT, W. B. and E. J. CROSSMAN
1962   A list of Ontario fishes. Toronto, Royal Ontario Museum, Dept. of Fishes. 6 pp.
1969   Checklist of Canadian freshwater fishes with keys for identification. Life Sciences Miscellaneous Publications. Toronto, Royal Ontario Museum. 104 pp.
1973a   Freshwater fishes of Canada. Bulletin of the Fisheries Research Board of Canada 184. 966 pp.
1973b   Freshwater fishes of Canada. Bulletin of the Fisheries Research Board of Canada 184. 966 pp. (1979 Reprint with additional information).

SLASTENENKO, E. P.
1958   The freshwater fishes of Canada. Toronto, Kiev Press. 383 pp.

SMALL, H. B.
1883   Fishes of the Ottawa district. Transactions of the Ottawa Field Naturalists Club 4, 1882–1885:31–47.

STRICKLAND, D.
1988   Fishing in Algonquin Park. Whitney, The Friends of Algonquin Park. 31 pp.

TONER, G. C.
1933   Annotated list of fishes of Georgian Bay. Copeia 1933(3):133–40.
1937   Preliminary studies of the fishes of eastern Ontario. Bulletin of the Eastern Ontario Fish and Game Protection Association, Supplement 2. 24 pp.

URE, G. P.
1858   The handbook of Toronto. Toronto, Lovel and Gibson. 272 pp.

WRIGHT, R. R.
1892   Preliminary report on the fish and fisheries of Ontario. *In* Ontario Game and Fish Commission, Commissioners' Report. Toronto, Warwick and Sons, pp. 419–475.

INDEX TO SCIENTIFIC AND COMMON NAMES

Each species, subspecies, or hybrid is listed alphabetically by scientific name, common name, and common name in reverse order (e.g., perch, yellow). Family names, scientific (in capital letters) and common, are listed alphabetically. The page number in bold represents the location of the distribution map. All other page numbers represent location in text and/or checklist.

Acipenser fulvescens 14, **25**
ACIPENSERIDAE 14
Alaska blackfish 17
alewife 14, **33**
Alosa pseudoharengus 14, **33**
Alosa sapidissima 14, **34**
Ambloplites rupestris 18, **134**
Ameiurus melas 16, **86**, 163
Ameiurus natalis 16, **87**, 163
Ameiurus nebulosus 16, **88**, 163
American brook lamprey 14, **23**
American eel 14, **32**
American shad 14, **34**
Amia calva 14, **29**
AMIIDAE 14
Ammocrypta pellucida 19, **145**
Anguilla rostrata 14, **32**
ANGUILLIDAE 14
Apeltes quadracus 18, **123**
Aplodinotus grunniens 19, **161**
Arctic char 17, **114**
Arctic grayling 17
Astronotus ocellatus 19
ATHERINIDAE 18
Atlantic salmon 17, **112**
Aurora trout 17, **116**

banded darter 10
banded killifish 18, **120**
bass,
  largemouth 19, **142**
  rock 18, **134**
  smallmouth 19, **141**
  white 18, **133**
bigeye chub 10
bigmouth buffalo 16
bigmouth shiner 10
black buffalo 16
black bullhead 16, **86**
black crappie 19, **144**
black redhorse 16, **82**
blackchin shiner 15, **58**

blackfin cisco 17, **103**
blackfish, Alaska 17
blacknose dace 15, **70**
blacknose shiner 15, **59**
blackside darter 19, **156**
blackstripe topminnow 18, **121**
bloater 17, **100**
blue pike 19, **159**
bluegill 19, **139**
bluntnose minnow 15, **68**
bowfin 14, **29**
Bowfins 14
brassy minnow 15, **44**
bridle shiner 15, **56**
brindled madtom 16, **92**
brook silverside 18, **122**
brook stickleback 18, **124**
brook trout 8, 17, **115**
brown bullhead 16, **88**
brown trout 17, **113**
buffalo,
  bigmouth 16
  black 16
bullhead,
  black 16, **86**
  brown 16, **88**
  yellow 16, **87**
Bullhead Catfishes 16
burbot 18, **119**

Campostoma anomalum 14, **36**
Carassius auratus 14, **37**
carp,
  common 15, **41**
  grass 14
Carpiodes cyprinus 15, **74**
Carps and Minnows 14
catfish,
  channel 16, **89**
  flathead 16
CATOSTOMIDAE 8, 15
Catostomus catostomus 15, **75**

Catostomus commersoni 16, **76**
central mudminnow 17, **96**
central stoneroller 14, **36**
CENTRARCHIDAE 8, 18
chain pickerel 10
channel catfish 16, **89**
channel darter 19, **155**
char, Arctic 17, **114**
CHARACIDAE 16
Characins 16
cherry salmon 17
chinook salmon 17, **109**
chub,
  bigeye 10
  creek 15, **72**
  gravel 15, **42**
  hornyhead 15, **51**
  lake 14, **39**
  river 15, **52**
  silver 15, **49**
chubsucker, lake 16, **77**
chum salmon 17
CICHLIDAE 19
Cichlids 19
Cichlosoma managuense 19
cisco 17, **98**
cisco,
  blackfin 17, **103**
  deepwater 17, **101**
  shortjaw 17, **105**
  shortnose 17, **104**
Clinostomus elongatus 14, **38**
CLUPEIDAE 14
Codfishes 18
coho salmon 17, **107**
Colossoma bidens 16
common carp 15, **41**
common shiner 15, **47**
Coregonus alpenae 163
Coregonus artedi 17, **98**
Coregonus clupeaformis 17, **99**
Coregonus hoyi 17, **100**
Coregonus johannae 17, **101**
Coregonus kiyi 17, **102**
Coregonus nigripinnis 17, **103**
Coregonus reighardi 17, **104**
Coregonus zenithicus 17, **105**, 163
COTTIDAE 8, 18
Cottus bairdi 18, **127**
Cottus cognatus 18, **128**
Cottus ricei 18, **129**
Couesius plumbeus 14, **39**

crappie,
  black 19, **144**
  white 19, **143**
creek chub 15, **72**
Ctenopharyngodon idella 14
Culaea inconstans 18, **124**
cutlips minnow 15, **43**
CYCLOPTERIDAE 18
Cyclopterus lumpus 18
Cyprinella spiloptera 14, **40**, 163
CYPRINIDAE 8, 14
CYPRINODONTIDAE 18
Cyprinus carpio 15, **41**

dace,
  blacknose 15, **70**
  finescale 15, **67**
  longnose 15, **71**
  northern redbelly 15, **66**
  pearl 15, **50**
  redside 14, **38**
  southern redbelly 10
Dallia pectoralis 17
darter,
  banded 10
  blackside 19, **156**
  channel 19, **155**
  eastern sand 19, **145**
  fantail 19, **149**
  greenside 19, **146**
  Iowa 19, **148**
  johnny 19, **151**
  least 19, **150**
  orangethroat 10
  rainbow 19, **147**
  river 19, **157**
  tessellated 19, **152**
  variegate 10
deepwater cisco 17, **101**
deepwater sculpin 18, **131**
Dorosoma cepedianum 14, **35**
drum, freshwater 19, **161**
Drums 19

eastern sand darter 19, **145**
eastern silvery minnow 15, **45**
eel, American 14, **32**
emerald shiner 15, **55**
Erimystax x-punctatus 15, **42**, 163
Erimyzon sucetta 16, **77**
ESOCIDAE 16
Esox americanus americanus 10
Esox americanus vermiculatus 16, **93**
Esox lucius 8, 16, **94**

Esox lucius X *Esox masquinongy*   16
Esox masquinongy   8, 16, **95**
Esox niger   10
Etheostoma blennioides   19, **146**
Etheostoma caeruleum   19, **147**
Etheostoma exile   19, **148**
Etheostoma flabellare   19, **149**
Etheostoma microperca   19, **150**
Etheostoma nigrum   19, **151**
Etheostoma olmstedi   19, **152**
Etheostoma spectabile   10
Etheostoma variatum   10
Etheostoma zonale   10
European flounder   20
Exoglossum laurae   10
Exoglossum maxillingua   15, **43**

fallfish   10, 15, **73**
fantail darter   19, **149**
fathead minnow   15, **69**
finescale dace   15, **67**
flathead catfish   16
Florida gar   14
flounder, European   20
fourhorn sculpin   18, **130**
fourspine stickleback   18, **123**
freshwater drum   19, **161**
Freshwater Eels   14
Fundulus diaphanus   18, **120**
Fundulus notatus   18, **121**

GADIDAE   18
Gambusia affinis   18
gar,
   Florida   14
   longnose   14, **28**
   spotted   14, **27**
Gars   14
GASTEROSTEIDAE   18
Gasterosteus aculeatus   18, **125**
ghost shiner   15, **57**
gizzard shad   14, **35**
Gobies   19
GOBIIDAE   19
goby,
   round   19
   tubenose   10
golden redhorse   16, **83**
golden shiner   15, **53**
goldeye   14, **30**
goldfish   14, **37**
grass carp   14
grass pickerel   16, **93**
gravel chub   15, **42**

grayling, Arctic   17
greater redhorse   16, **85**
green sunfish   18, **135**
greenside darter   19, **146**
guapote, jaguar   19
Gymnocephalus cernuus   19

herring, lake   17, **98**
Herrings   14
Hiodon alosoides   14, **30**
Hiodon tergisus   14, **31**
HIODONTIDAE   14
hornyhead chub   15, **51**
Hybognathus hankinsoni   15, **44**
Hybognathus regius   15, **45**
Hybopsis storeriana   163
Hybopsis x-punctata   163
Hypentelium nigricans   16, **78**

Ichthyomyzon fossor   14, **21**
Ichthyomyzon unicuspis   14, **22**
ICTALURIDAE   16
Ictalurus melas   163
Ictalurus natalis   163
Ictalurus nebulosus   163
Ictalurus punctatus   16, **89**
Ictiobus cyprinellus   16
Ictiobus niger   16
Iowa darter   19, **148**

jaguar guapote   19
johnny darter   19, **151**

killifish, banded   18, **120**
Killifishes   18
kiyi   17, **102**

Labidesthes sicculus   18, **122**
lake chub   14, **39**
lake chubsucker   16, **77**
lake herring   17, **98**
lake sturgeon   14, **25**
lake trout   8, 17, **117**
lake whitefish   17, **99**
Lampetra appendix   14, **23**
lamprey,
   American brook   14, **23**
   northern brook   14, **21**
   sea   14, **24**
   silver   14, **22**
Lampreys   14
largemouth bass   19, **142**
least darter   19, **150**
LEPISOSTEIDAE   14
Lepisosteus oculatus   14, **27**

Lepisosteus osseus   14, **28**
Lepisosteus platyrhynchus   14
Lepomis cyanellus   18, **135**
Lepomis gibbosus   19, **136**
Lepomis gulosus   19, **137**
Lepomis humilis   19, **138**
Lepomis macrochirus   19, **139**
Lepomis megalotis   10, 19, **140**
Lepomis microlophus   10
Leucichthys   4
Livebearers   18
logperch   19, **154**
longear sunfish   10, 19, **140**
longnose dace   15, **71**
longnose gar   14, **28**
longnose sucker   15, **75**
LORICARIIDAE   16
Lota lota   18, **119**
lumpfish   18
Luxilus chrysocephalus   15, **46**, 163
Luxilus cornutus   15, **47**, 163
Lythrurus umbratilis   15, **48**, 163

Macrhybopsis storeriana   15, **49**, 163
madtom,
   brindled   16, **92**
   margined   16
   northern   16
   tadpole   16, **91**
Margariscus margarita   15, **50**, 163
margined madtom   16
Micropterus dolomieu   19, **141**
Micropterus salmoides   19, **142**
mimic shiner   15, **64**
minnow,
   bluntnose   15, **68**
   brassy   15, **44**
   cutlips   15, **43**
   eastern silvery   15, **45**
   fathead   15, **69**
   pugnose   15, **65**
   silverjaw   10
   suckermouth   10
   tonguetied   10
Minytrema melanops   16, **79**
mooneye   14, **31**
Mooneyes   14
Morone americana   10, 18, **132**
Morone chrysops   18, **133**
mosquitofish   18
mottled sculpin   18, **127**
Moxostoma anisurum   16, **80**
Moxostoma carinatum   16, **81**
Moxostoma duquesnei   16, **82**

Moxostoma erythrurum   16, **83**
Moxostoma macrolepidotum   16, **84**
Moxostoma valenciennesi   16, **85**
mudminnow, central   17, **96**
Mudminnows   17
muskellunge   8, 16, **95**
muskellunge, tiger   8, 16
Myoxocephalus quadricornis   18, **130**
Myoxocephalus thompsoni   18, **131**

Neogobius melanostomus   19
ninespine stickleback   18, **126**
Nocomis biguttatus   15, **51**
Nocomis micropogon   15, **52**
northern brook lamprey   14, **21**
northern hognose sucker   16, **78**
northern madtom   16
northern pike   8, 16, **94**
northern redbelly dace   15, **66**
Notemigonus crysoleucas   15, **53**
Notropis amblops   10
Notropis anogenus   15, **54**
Notropis atherinoides   15, **55**
Notropis bifrenatus   15, **56**
Notropis blennius   10
Notropis buccatus   10
Notropis buchanani   15, **57**
Notropis chrysocephalus   163
Notropis cornutus   163
Notropis dorsalis   10
Notropis emiliae   163
Notropis heterodon   15, **58**
Notropis heterolepis   15, **59**
Notropis hudsonius   15, **60**
Notropis photogenis   15, **61**
Notropis rubellus   15, **62**
Notropis spilopterus   163
Notropis stramineus   15, **63**
Notropis texanus   9, 10
Notropis umbratilis   163
Notropis volucellus   15, **64**
Noturus flavus   16, **90**
Noturus gyrinus   16, **91**
Noturus insignis   16
Noturus miurus   16, **92**
Noturus stigmosus   16

Oncorhynchus gorbuscha   17, **106**
Oncorhynchus keta   17
Oncorhynchus kisutch   17, **107**
Oncorhynchus masou   17
Oncorhynchus mykiss   8, 17, **108**, 163
Oncorhynchus nerka   17
Oncorhynchus tshawytscha   17, **109**

173

Opsopoeodus emiliae 15, **65**, 163
orangespotted sunfish 19, **138**
orangethroat darter 10
oscar 19
OSMERIDAE 17
Osmerus mordax 17, **97**

pacu 16
paddlefish 14, **26**
Paddlefishes 14
Panaque nigrolineatus 16
panaque, royal 16
pearl dace 15, **50**
Perca flavescens 8, 19, **153**
perch,
    white 10, 18, **132**
    yellow 8, 19, **153**
Perches 19
PERCICHTHYIDAE 18
PERCIDAE 19
Percina caprodes 19, **154**
Percina copelandi 19, **155**
Percina maculata 19, **156**
Percina shumardi 19, **157**
PERCOPSIDAE 18
Percopsis omiscomaycus 18, **118**
Petromyzon marinus 14, **24**
PETROMYZONTIDAE 14
Phenacobious mirabilis 10
Phoxinus eos 15, **66**
Phoxinus erythrogaster 10
Phoxinus neogaeus 15, **67**
pickerel,
    chain 10
    grass 16, **93**
    redfin 10
pike,
    blue 19, **159**
    northern 8, 16, **94**
Pikes 16
Pimephales notatus 15, **68**
Pimephales promelas 15, **69**
pink salmon 17, **106**
Platichthys flesus 20
PLEURONECTIDAE 20
POECILIIDAE 18
Polyodon spathula 14, **26**
POLYODONTIDAE 14
Pomoxis annularis 19, **143**
Pomoxis nigromaculatus 19, **144**
Prosopium coulteri 17, **110**
Prosopium cylindraceum 17, **111**
Proterorhinus marmoratus 10
pugnose minnow 15, **65**

pugnose shiner 15, **54**
pumpkinseed 19, **136**
Pungitius pungitius 18, **126**
pygmy whitefish 17, **110**
Pylodictis olivaris 16

quillback 15, **74**

rainbow darter 19, **147**
rainbow smelt 17, **97**
rainbow trout 8, 17, **108**
redear sunfish 10
redfin pickerel 10
redfin shiner 15, **48**
redhorse,
    black 16, **82**
    golden 16, **83**
    greater 16, **85**
    river 16, **81**
    shorthead 16, **84**
    silver 16, **80**
redside dace 14, **38**
Rhinichthys atratulus 15, **70**
Rhinichthys cataractae 15, **71**
Righteye Flounders 20
river chub 15, **52**
river darter 19, **157**
river redhorse 16, **81**
river shiner 10
rock bass 18, **134**
rosyface shiner 15, **62**
round goby 19
round whitefish 17, **111**
royal panaque 16
rudd 15
ruffe 19

Salmo gairdneri 163
Salmo salar 17, **112**
Salmo trutta 17, **113**
salmon,
    Atlantic 17, **112**
    cherry 17
    chinook 17, **109**
    chum 17
    coho 17, **107**
    pink 17, **106**
    sockeye 17
SALMONIDAE 8, 17
Salvelinus alpinus 17, **114**
Salvelinus fontinalis fontinalis 8, 17, **115**
Salvelinus fontinalis timagamiensis 8, 17, **116**

Salvelinus fontinalis X *Salvelinus namaycush*   17
Salvelinus namaycush   8, 17, **117**
sand shiner   15, **63**
sauger   18, **158**
Scardinius erythrophthalmus   15
SCIAENIDAE   19
sculpin,
   deepwater   18, **131**
   fourhorn   18, **130**
   mottled   18, **127**
   slimy   18, **128**
   spoonhead   18, **129**
Sculpins   18
sea lamprey   14, **24**
Semotilus atromaculatus   15, **72**
Semotilus corporalis   10, 15, **73**
Semotilus margarita   163
shad.
   American   14, **34**
   gizzard   14, **35**
shiner,
   bigmouth   10
   blackchin   15, **58**
   blacknose   15, **59**
   bridle   15, **56**
   common   15, **47**
   emerald   15, **55**
   ghost   15, **57**
   golden   15, **53**
   mimic   15, **64**
   pugnose   15, **54**
   redfin   15, **48**
   river   10
   rosyface   15, **62**
   sand   15, **63**
   silver   15, **61**
   spotfin   14, **40**
   spottail   15, **60**
   striped   15, **46**
   weed   10
shorthead redhorse   16, **84**
shortjaw cisco   17, **105**
shortnose cisco   17, **104**
silver chub   15, **49**
silver lamprey   14, **22**
silver redhorse   16, **80**
silver shiner   15, **61**
silverjaw minnow   10
silverside, brook   18, **122**
Silversides   18
slimy sculpin   18, **128**
smallmouth bass   19, **141**
smelt, rainbow   17, **97**

Smelts   17
Snailfishes   18
sockeye salmon   17
southern redbelly dace   10
splake   8, 17
spoonhead sculpin   18, **129**
spotfin shiner   14, **40**
spottail shiner   15, **60**
spotted gar   14, **27**
spotted sucker   16, **79**
stickleback,
   brook   18, **124**
   fourspine   18, **123**
   ninespine   18, **126**
   threespine   18, **125**
Sticklebacks   18
Stizostedion canadense   19, **158**
Stizostedion vitreum glaucum   19, **159**
Stizostedion vitreum vitreum   19, **160**
stonecat   16, **90**
stoneroller, central   14, **36**
striped shiner   15, **46**
sturgeon, lake   14, **25**
Sturgeons   14
sucker,
   longnose   15, **75**
   northern hognose   16, **78**
   spotted   16, **79**
   white   16, **76**
Suckermouth Catfishes   16
suckermouth minnow   10
Suckers   15
sunfish,
   green   18, **135**
   longear   10, 19, **140**
   orangespotted   19, **138**
   redear   10
Sunfishes   18

tadpole madtom   16, **91**
Temperate Basses   18
tessellated darter   19, **152**
threespine stickleback   18, **125**
Thymallus arcticus   17
tiger muskellunge   8, 16
tonguetied minnow   10
topminnow, blackstripe   18, **121**
trout,
   Aurora   17, **116**
   brook   8, 17, **115**
   brown   17, **113**
   lake   8, 17, **117**
   rainbow   8, 17, **108**
trout-perch   18, **118**

Trout-perches   18
Trouts   17
tubenose goby   10

Umbra limi   17, **96**
UMBRIDAE   17

variegate darter   10

walleye   19, **160**
warmouth   19, **137**
weed shiner   10

white bass   18, **133**
white crappie   19, **143**
white perch   10, 18, **132**
white sucker   16, **76**
whitefish,
   lake   17, **99**
   pygmy   17, **110**
   round   17, **111**

yellow bullhead   16, **87**
yellow perch   8, 19, **153**